CHARLES III
THE MAKING OF A KING

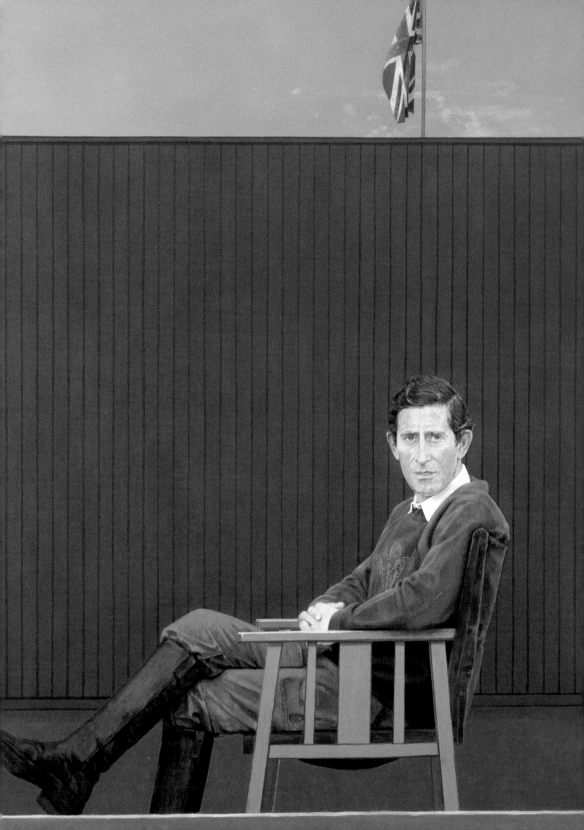

CHARLES III
THE MAKING OF A KING

INTRODUCTION BY ALISON SMITH

NATIONAL PORTRAIT GALLERY, LONDON

CONTENTS

INTRODUCTION

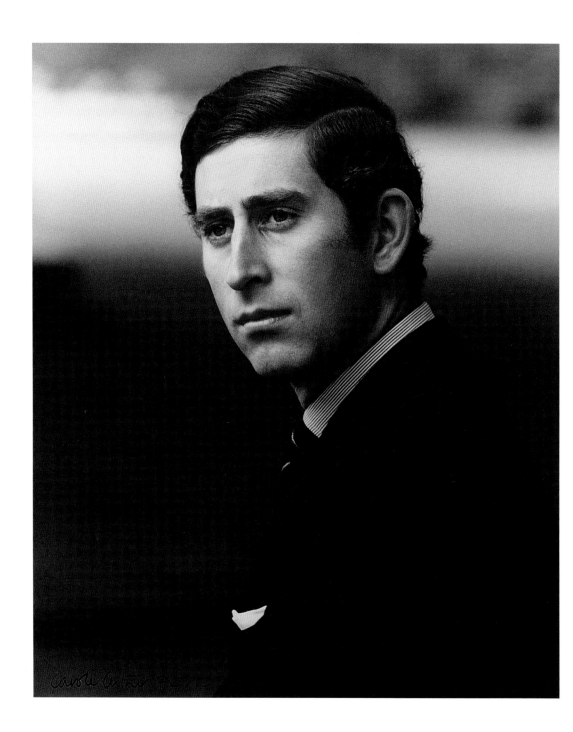

CHARLES III
THE
MAKING
OF
A KING

Alison Smith

When King Charles acceded to the throne on 8 September 2022, he had earned the reputation of being the longest-waiting heir apparent in the history of the United Kingdom. The many photographs that chart the course of his life over 73 years testify to the various ways he used those decades to develop other interests alongside his official duties. The long interlude was not always easy or without challenges, for as one of the 'baby boomer' generation, he came to maturity at a time when post-war austerity and deference gave way to freedom of expression with social reforms ushering in a more tolerant yet outwardly spoken society. At the same time, technological developments encouraged greater media scrutiny of public figures than ever before. Against this background, Charles stands out in the history of the British monarchy for being an activist royal, often taking his cue from politics rather than the paradigm of the disinterested public servant upheld by his mother Queen Elizabeth II, and grandfather George VI. Viewed chronologically, the images in this book reveal how an adored child evolved into a rather gauche teenager before becoming an independently-minded adult driven by private passions that include a deep interest in inter-faith and environmental issues. Some of the causes Charles has espoused, such as alternative medicine and climate change, were once considered eccentric but are now widely accepted, and it is perhaps only in recent years that he has come into his own as a man fully able to hold his many private interests in balance with his public constitutional duties. This has prompted much speculation about how he will adapt to his new role.

Portraits will be key in upholding the symbolic ideal of monarchy while foregrounding the King as a person in all his complexity. The tension between these two approaches inevitably raises questions of influence and appropriation. What images of kingship will Charles and his artists draw on in crystallising his reign in the public mind? Exemplars might include portraits of earlier kings who also had to wait a long time before taking the throne. But it is highly unlikely Charles will adopt the swaggering personae George IV and Edward VII, for example, projected at the time of their coronations. Anthony van Dyck's portraits of Charles I may communicate more appealing qualities of sensitivity and feeling, but that ill-fated monarch's association with absolute power attracts little sympathy today. As the historian David Cannadine reminds us, the modern model of constitutional monarchy is a rather emasculated ideal in that, since Queen Victoria, it has valued traditionally 'feminine' values of morality and domesticity above those of national leadership and military prowess. Of all his male antecedents, Charles has perhaps most in common with George III, who was also unusually intellectual for a royal and likewise concerned for the environment, his agricultural interests earning him the nickname Farmer George. But the classicising iconography of the eighteenth century would be hard to retread. In collaborating with artists and photographers, it seems likely that Charles will favour those who are able to convey the stability associated with monarchy while admitting a degree of spontaneity in acknowledgement of the qualities we value in portraiture today.

The National Portrait Gallery has around 170 portraits of the King in its collection. None of these is a sculptural work and there is only one painting in which he appears as the sole subject. Although the absence of other paintings may seem odd given Charles's love of art, we should remember that there were few official painted portraits of the late

Queen before her accession. Bryan Organ's portrait, commissioned in 1980, a year before Charles's marriage to Lady Diana Spencer, is spare yet subtle. Isolated against a bare walled background, the Prince sits casual but alert as he turns to face the spectator in his polo clothes. The only sign of his royal identity is the Union Jack hanging limply in the background. The painting stands out among the many representations of Charles, its very simplicity anticipating the pared-down iconography he has chosen to adopt as King such as the new coins issued by the Royal Mint in which he is significantly not shown wearing a crown, the word *REX* standing in for the idea of kingship instead.

The overwhelming majority of portraits of the King in the National Portrait Gallery's collection are photographs, which is only to be expected given that photography is now the dominant medium for portraiture (overall photography represents some 68% of all the Gallery's collections). The relentless flow of images also bears witness to the fact that Charles has been in the public eye since he was a baby. As a group the photographs document the supportive role he played during his mother's long reign and chart key moments in his life, including his investiture as Prince of Wales and first marriage. Since becoming popular in the nineteenth century, photographs have been carefully utilised by generations of royals to foster and disseminate their public image, and the photographs of Charles are no exception. Most were made to communicate the rites of passage one would associate with a royal, from the happy family and marriage groupings to portraits of the Prince in various guises, military and civilian. As the official 'visual report' of monarchy, the images disclose little about his private life or provide insight as to what he might be feeling.

In the overall impression they leave of hard-working charm, they form part of the protective covering that has helped preserve the royal family's soft power over the years, distancing it from the international perception of national instability that has become particularly pervasive in recent years.

Over the course of his life Charles has been photographed by some of the most celebrated photographers of the day, including Cecil Beaton, Norman Parkinson, Terence Donovan, Bern Schwartz and Mario Testino. Photographers who were related to the royal family, like the Earl of Snowdon (husband to Charles's aunt Princess Margaret) and Patrick Lichfield (cousin of the Queen), often sought to capture the royals off-guard and to reveal a hidden side to their personality while never losing sight of their dignity. The occasional reference in these works to earlier imagery has helped underscore the idea of continuity across time. Beaton's delightful 1950 photograph of Princess Elizabeth giving a rather apprehensive Charles a piggyback (fig.3) is a deliberate reprise of a popular carte-de-visite of Princess Alexandra playing with Princess Louise in a similar manner in 1868 (fig.2). Snowdon's 1991 colour print of Charles and Diana enjoying a picnic with their sons, is a rather forced throwback to the type of conversation piece favoured by the English aristocracy in the eighteenth century, right down to the horse in the background and oak tree suggesting endurance. With hindsight the sheer contrivance and artificiality of the composition serves to underscore the pretence of harmonious family life at a time when the relationship between the couple was under strain.

In many photographs Charles stands dutifully facing the spectator. Sometimes he smiles and the

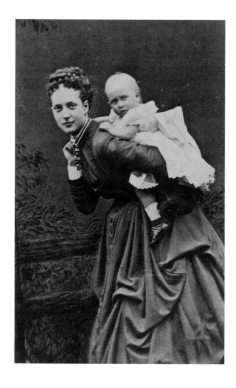

[FIG.2]
QUEEN ALEXANDRA AND PRINCESS LOUISE
W. & D. DOWNEY, SEPTEMBER 1868

Albumen carte-de-visite, 92 x 58mm
NPG x135624

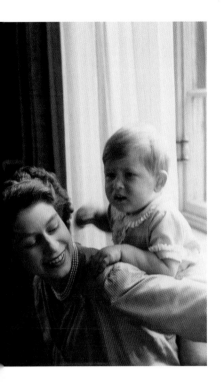

occasional hand gesture animates his presence to communicate an openness to his personality. Among the more compelling photographs are those that hint at a hinterland beyond the public persona. Carole Cutner's sensitive close-up colour print of the 26-year-old Prince manipulates light and shadow to suggest a rather thoughtful, perhaps anxious young man, inwardly bracing himself for the future (fig.1). What is apparent from all the photographs is the consistency in Charles's dress and deportment from the time he was a small boy right up to the present day. As an adult, he is invariably shown wearing classic double-breasted suits finished with a signature pocket square and flower in his buttonhole, the latter often blue to complement his eyes. This formal mode of dress has hardly changed across the decades and is immaculate down to the shoelaces (which according to some sources are ironed). Charles's dress speaks of a timeless, essentially British formality and serves to accentuate his face and profile which has gradually filled out over the years to make him appear more approachable as a person.

Anyone searching for the man behind the mask should look at some recent photographs that capture the more relaxed, caring and secure person who emerged following Charles's marriage to Camilla Parker Bowles, now Queen Consort, in 2005. One of the most appealing is the picture taken by Alexi Lubomirski of Charles and Camilla in the morning room at Clarence House in 2018. Seated in the lower right of the image, the couple appear to enjoy a private joke, seemingly unaware of the commanding figure of Muhammad Ali – tyrant of early nineteenth-century Egypt – who leans forward in the magnificent Gobelins tapestry on the wall behind them as if to tap

[FIG.3]
**PRINCESS ELIZABETH OF EDINBURGH AND
PRINCE CHARLES OF EDINBURGH**
CLARENCE HOUSE, LONDON
CECIL BEATON, SEPTEMBER 1950

Gelatin silver print, printed later, 245 x 178mm
NPG x29299

Camilla on the head. Hidden from view behind the sofa, the tapestry includes a rather gruesome scene depicting the massacre of Mamelukes in Cairo, but the couple are not at all disturbed by this: rather they sit at affectionate ease in each other's company. Camilla's hand on Charles's thigh adds an intimate touch, in delicate breach perhaps of the royal code of not touching in public.

In recent years, photographers have directed their cameras at the head of the King as if to emphasise the gravitas that comes with experience. Nadav Kander's monumental portrait, first published as the cover of a 2013 issue of *TIME* magazine, has become the prototype for this kind of image with its close-cropped composition and focus on the face alone (fig.4). Taken at Birkhall, the then Prince's private residence on the Balmoral estate in Aberdeenshire, it presents Charles as both a figurehead in the Tudor tradition, and as a man in all his complexity; in Kander's words 'as a sum of his experiences and aspirations'. Set against a dark background and lit to bring out the emotion in his eyes, the portrait conveys feeling without disturbing the sense of regal composure demanded by royal status. The blue cornflower in Charles's buttonhole adds a vivid touch of colour to the muted colour scheme while alluding to his appreciation of the natural world. It is a powerful and emotionally charged portrait offering insight into the intricate sense of self so often hidden in official portraits.

Now that he is King, it remains to be seen just how far Charles will continue to allow access to his inner world via portraiture. We wait to see if he will be even more forthcoming, or it may be that the performative side of the monarch's role will ultimately take precedence, as it has so often in the past.

[FIG. 4]
CHARLES, PRINCE OF WALES
BIRKHALL, ABERDEENSHIRE
NADAV KANDER, 20 AUGUST 2013

Chromogenic print, 1565 x 1220mm
NPG P1989

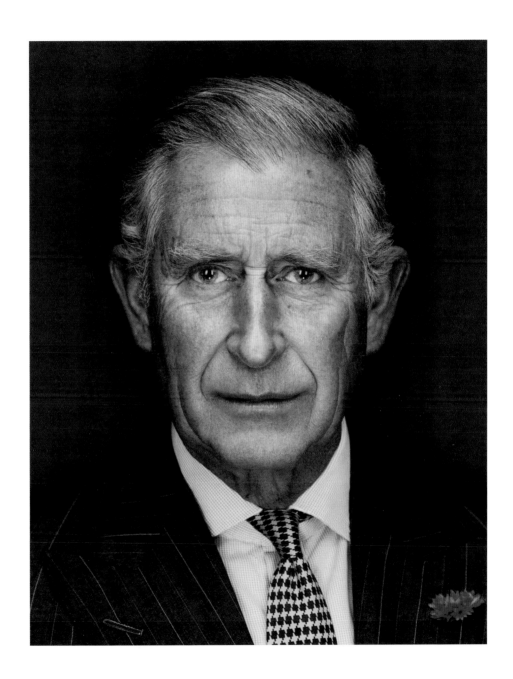

A PRINCE IS BORN

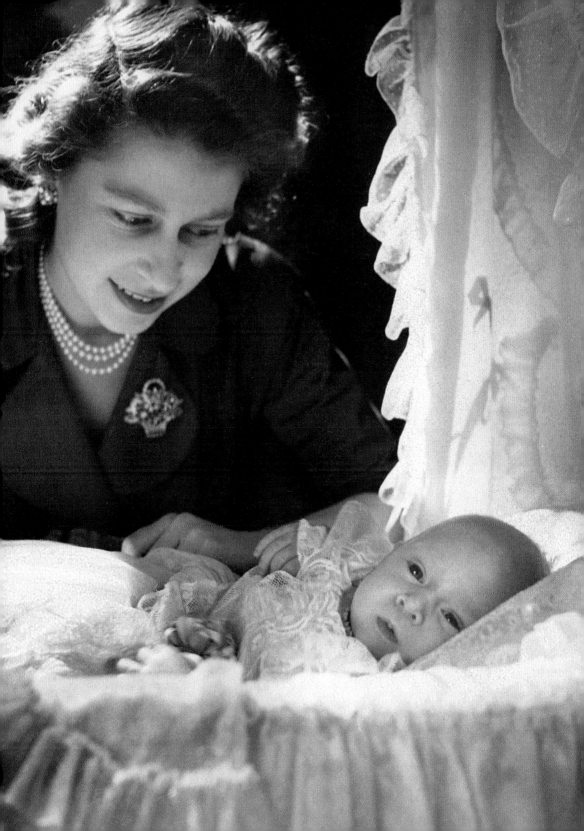

Previous spread
[1]
PRINCESS ELIZABETH OF EDINBURGH
AND PRINCE CHARLES OF EDINBURGH
CECIL BEATON, 14 DECEMBER 1948

Gelatin silver print, 205 x 196mm
NPG x29597

Charles Philip Arthur George was born at 9:14pm on 14 November 1948 at Buckingham Palace. He was the first child of Princess Elizabeth and Prince Philip, Duke of Edinburgh, and the first grandchild of King George VI and Queen Elizabeth, the Queen Mother. He was baptised a month later in the Music Room at Buckingham Palace by the Archbishop of Canterbury, Geoffrey Fisher, on 15 December 1948. He was known as Prince Charles of Edinburgh until 1958 when he was given the title Prince of Wales.

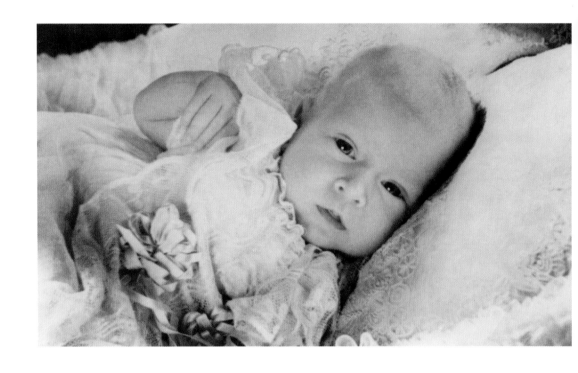

[2]
PRINCE CHARLES OF EDINBURGH
CECIL BEATON, PUBLISHED BY
RAPHAEL TUCK & SONS,
14 DECEMBER 1948

Gelatin silver postcard, 89 x 140mm
NPG x138068

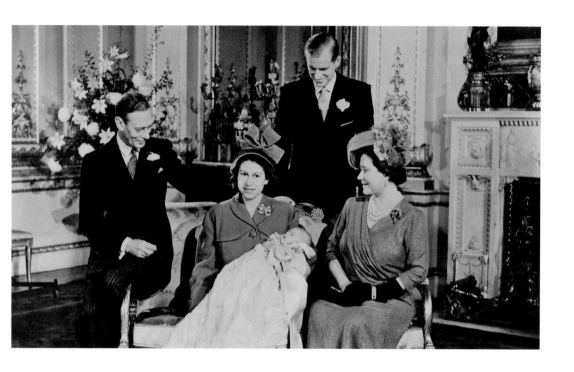

[3]

***KING GEORGE VI, PRINCESS ELIZABETH OF
EDINBURGH, PRINCE CHARLES OF EDINBURGH,
PRINCE PHILIP, DUKE OF EDINBURGH AND
QUEEN ELIZABETH, THE QUEEN MOTHER***
WHITE DRAWING ROOM, BUCKINGHAM
PALACE, LONDON
BARON, PUBLISHED BY RAPHAEL TUCK & SONS,
15 DECEMBER 1948

Gelatin silver postcard, 90 x 140mm
NPG x193001

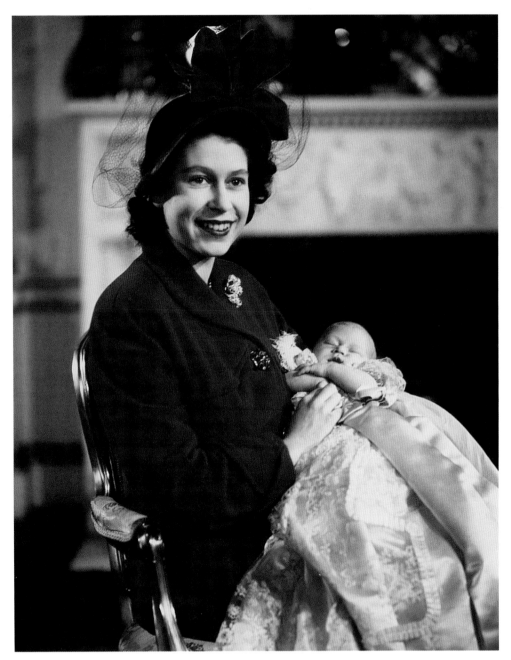

[4]
***PRINCESS ELIZABETH OF EDINBURGH AND PRINCE
CHARLES OF EDINBURGH***
WHITE DRAWING ROOM, BUCKINGHAM PALACE, LONDON
BARON, 15 DECEMBER 1948

Cibachrome print, 331 x 263mm
NPG x35386

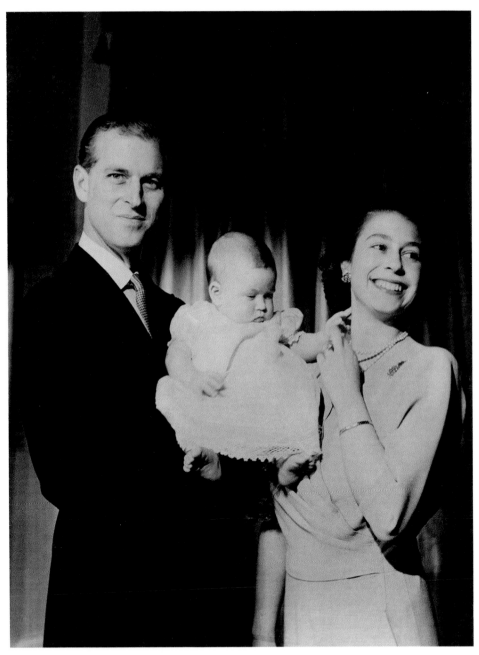

[5]
***PRINCE PHILIP, DUKE OF EDINBURGH, PRINCE
CHARLES OF EDINBURGH AND PRINCESS ELIZABETH
OF EDINBURGH***
BARON, PUBLISHED BY RAPHAEL TUCK & SONS, 1949

Gelatin silver postcard, 140 x 89mm
NPG x136406

Marcus Adams was widely acclaimed for his photographic portraits of children. Adams took his first official photographs of the Queen Mother and Princess Elizabeth in 1926 and continued photographing the royal family up until 1956. This portrait of Princess Elizabeth with Prince Charles was taken during Charles's first sitting with Adams at The Children's Studio, Dover Street, in London.

[6]
PRINCESS ELIZABETH OF EDINBURGH AND PRINCE CHARLES OF EDINBURGH
THE CHILDREN'S STUDIO, 43 DOVER
STREET, LONDON
MARCUS ADAMS, 26 OCTOBER 1949

Cibachrome print, 331 x 258mm
NPG x35394

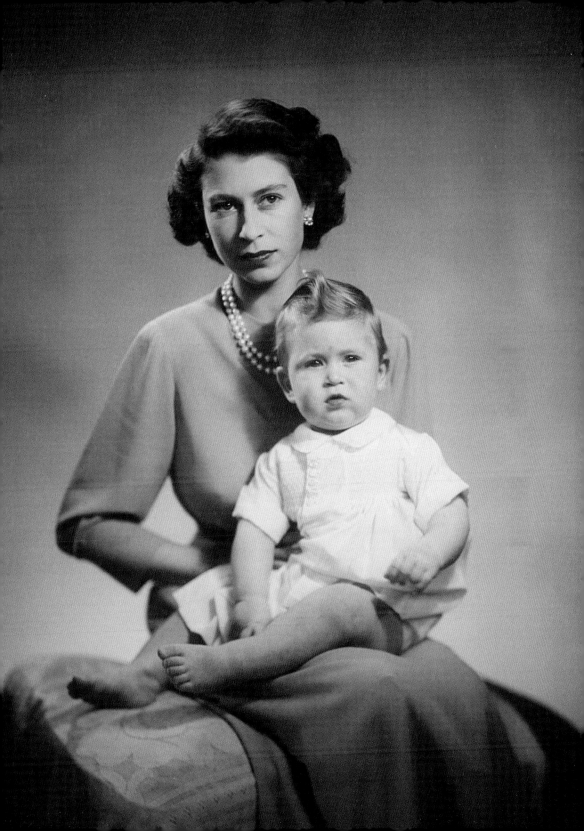

[7]
PRINCESS ELIZABETH OF EDINBURGH
AND PRINCE CHARLES OF EDINBURGH
CLARENCE HOUSE, LONDON
CECIL BEATON, SEPTEMBER 1950

Gelatin silver print, printed later,
245 x 178mm
NPG x29299

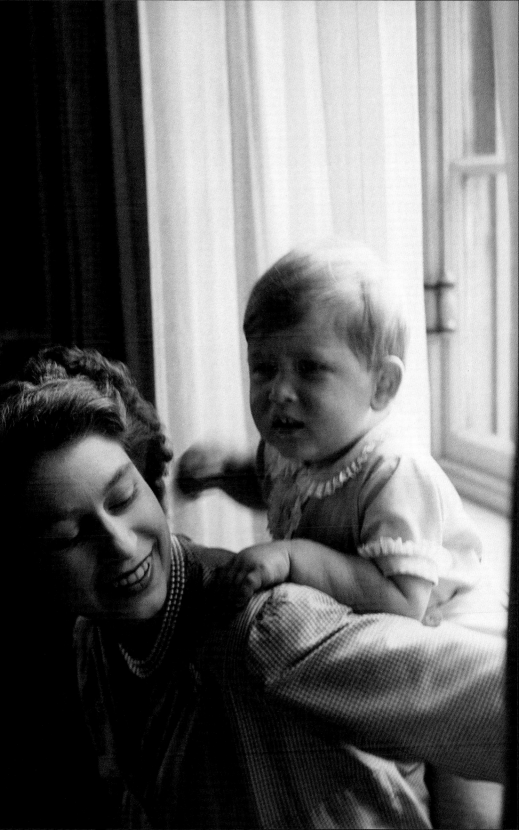

Anne Elizabeth Alice Louise, the second child and only daughter of Princess Elizabeth and Prince Philip, Duke of Edinburgh, was born on 15 August 1950 at Clarence House. Anne was christened in the Music Room at Buckingham Palace on 21 October 1950 by the Archbishop of York, Cyril Garbett. She has been known as Anne, Princess Royal since 1987.

[8]
PRINCE CHARLES OF EDINBURGH AND PRINCESS ANNE
CECIL BEATON, PUBLISHED BY RAPHAEL TUCK & SONS, SEPTEMBER 1950

Gelatin silver postcard, 140 x 91mm
NPG x138108

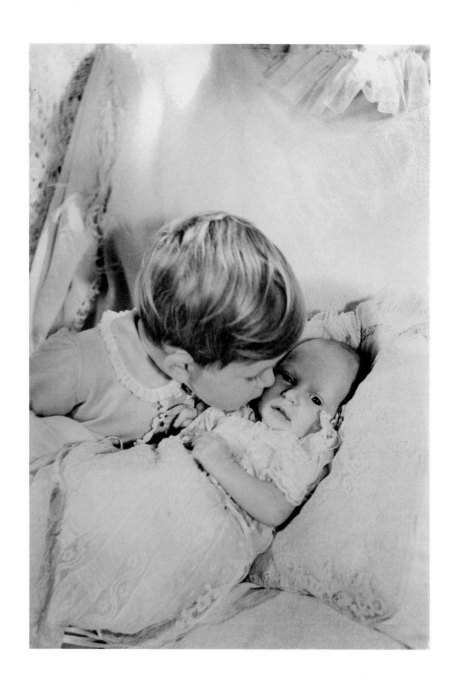

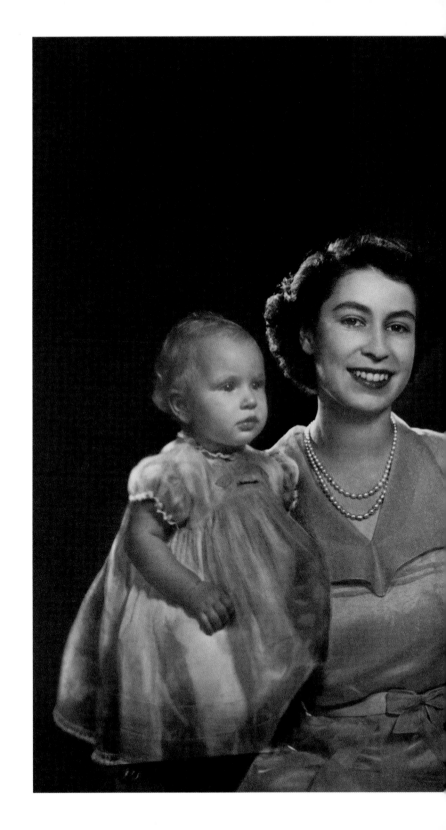

[9]
'THE ROYAL FAMILY'
YOUSUF KARSH, 1951

Gelatin silver print,
273 x 352mm
NPG P347

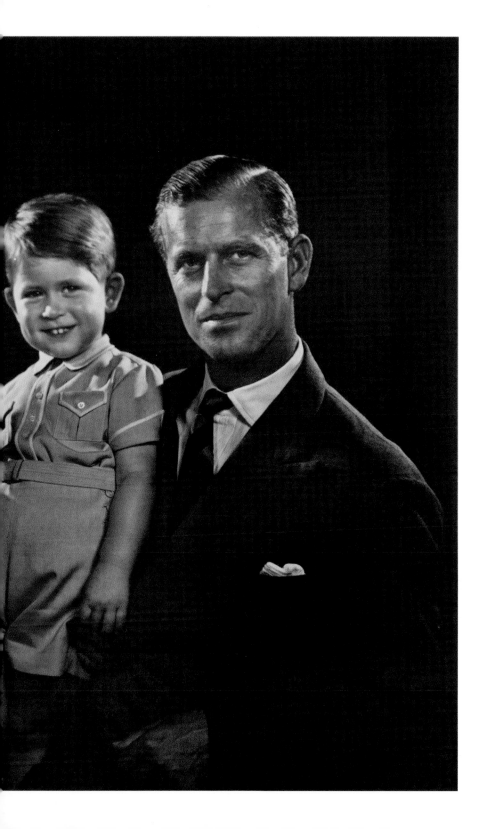

PRINCE CHARLES OF EDINBURGH
MARCUS ADAMS, 1951

Gelatin silver print, 215 x 164mm
NPG x198509

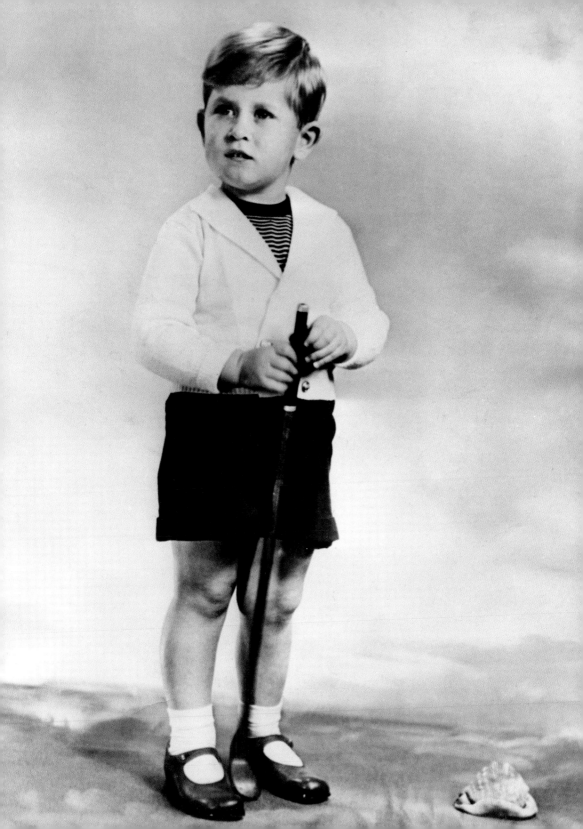

[11]
PRINCESS ELIZABETH OF EDINBURGH WITH
HER PARENTS, HUSBAND, SON AND SISTER
BALMORAL CASTLE, ABERDEENSHIRE
JAMES REID, AUGUST 1951

Gelatin silver print, 56 x 81mm
NPG x35705

[12]
KING GEORGE VI AND PRINCE CHARLES
OF EDINBURGH
BUCKINGHAM PALACE, LONDON
PUBLISHED BY RAPHAEL TUCK & SONS,
NOVEMBER 1951, PUBLISHED 1952

Gelatin silver postcard, 138 x 91mm
NPG x193002

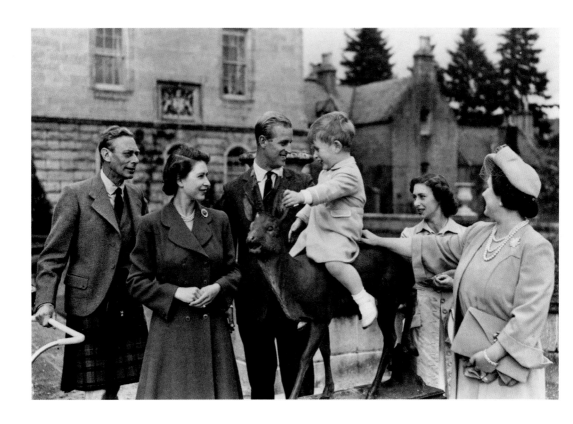

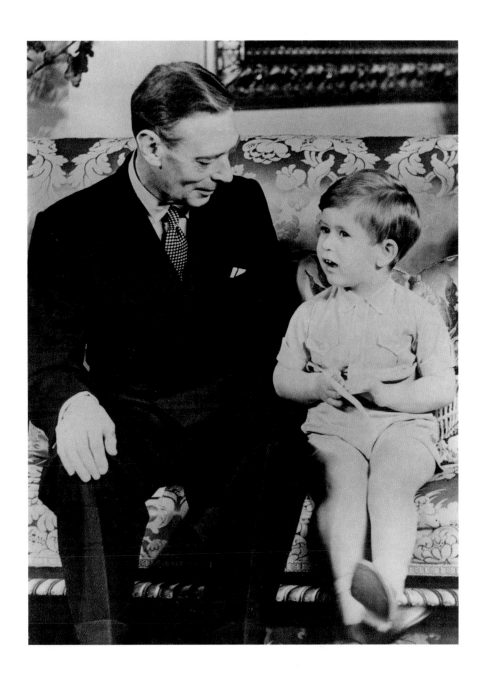

THE
NEW HEIR
APPARENT

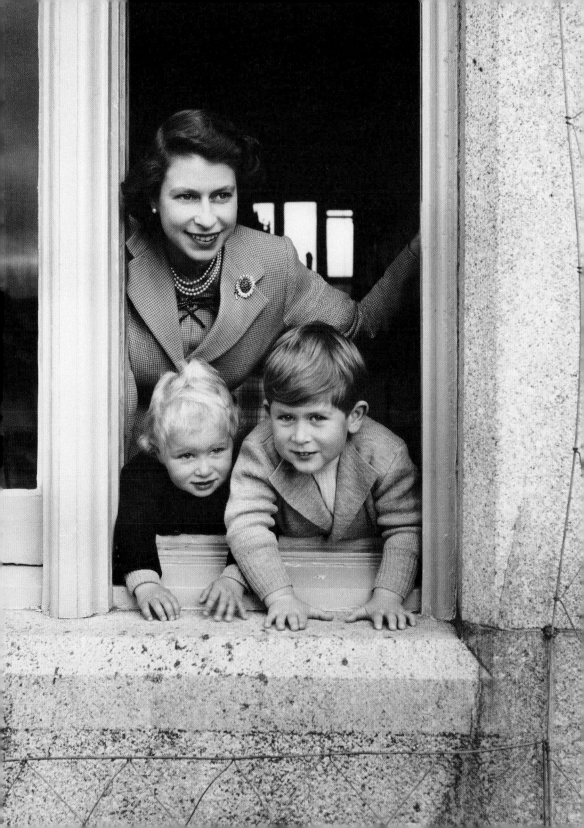

After the death of his grandfather and the accession of his mother as Queen Elizabeth II in 1952, Prince Charles became the heir apparent. Elizabeth's coronation took place just over a year later on 2 June 1953 at Westminster Abbey, London. As the monarch's eldest son, Charles automatically assumed the titles Duke of Cornwall, Duke of Rothesay, Earl of Carrick, Baron of Renfrew, Lord of the Isles, and Prince and Great Steward of Scotland. Charles was given the title Prince of Wales and Earl of Chester on 26 July 1958.

Over 30 years, husband-and-wife team
Lisa and Jimmy Sheridan recorded
13 photographic sessions with three
generations of the royal family, including
photographing the Queen with her
children at Balmoral Castle in 1952 and
Windsor Castle in 1954.

[14]
PRINCESS ANNE, QUEEN ELIZABETH II, PRINCE
PHILIP, DUKE OF EDINBURGH AND PRINCE
CHARLES OF EDINBURGH
BALMORAL CASTLE, ABERDEENSHIRE
STUDIO LISA (LISA SHERIDAN), 28 SEPTEMBER 1952

Gelatin silver print, 495 x 395mm
NPG P1613

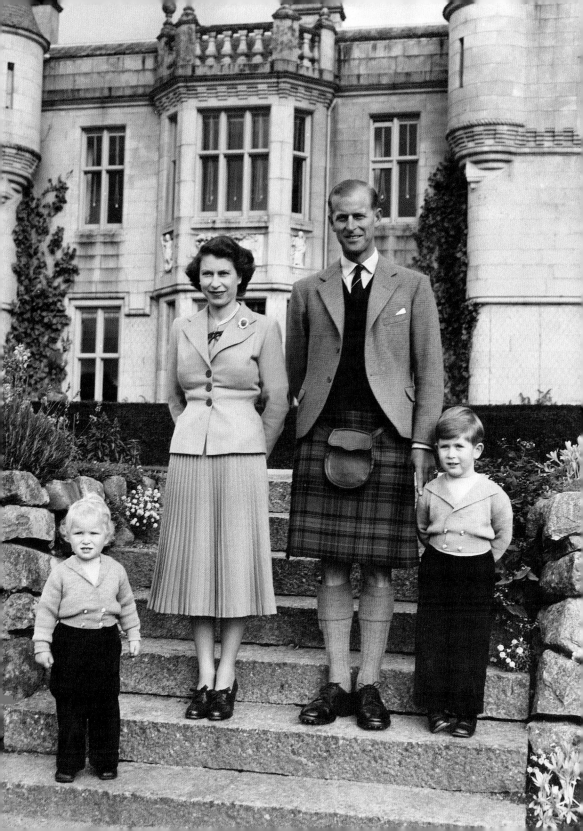

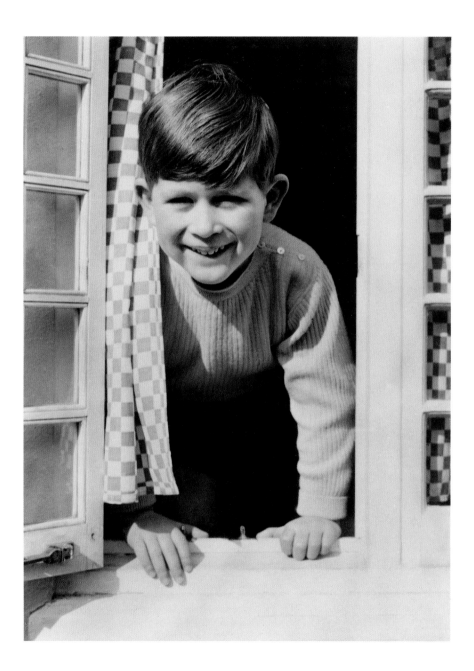

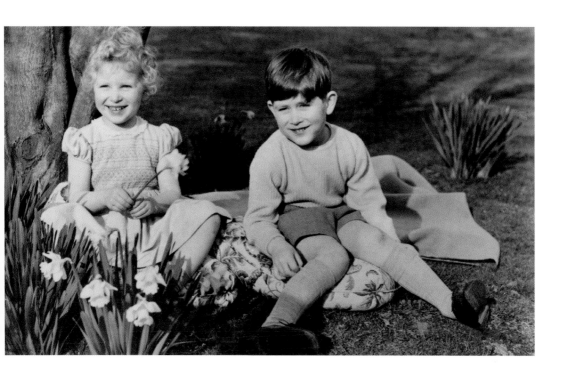

[15]
PRINCE CHARLES OF EDINBURGH
ROYAL LODGE, WINDSOR, BERKSHIRE
STUDIO LISA (LISA SHERIDAN), PUBLISHED BY
RAPHAEL TUCK & SONS, 23 APRIL 1954

Gelatin silver postcard, 140 x 89mm
NPG x138097

[16]
PRINCESS ANNE AND PRINCE CHARLES OF EDINBURGH
GARDEN OF THE ROYAL LODGE, WINDSOR, BERKSHIRE
STUDIO LISA (LISA SHERIDAN), PUBLISHED BY
RAPHAEL TUCK & SONS, 23 APRIL 1954

Gelatin silver postcard, 90 x 140mm
NPG x138100

[17]
**PRINCE CHARLES OF EDINBURGH, QUEEN
ELIZABETH II AND PRINCESS ANNE**
THE CHILDREN'S STUDIO, 43 DOVER STREET,
LONDON
MARCUS ADAMS, 6 NOVEMBER 1954

Cibachrome print, 482 x 382mm
NPG P1408

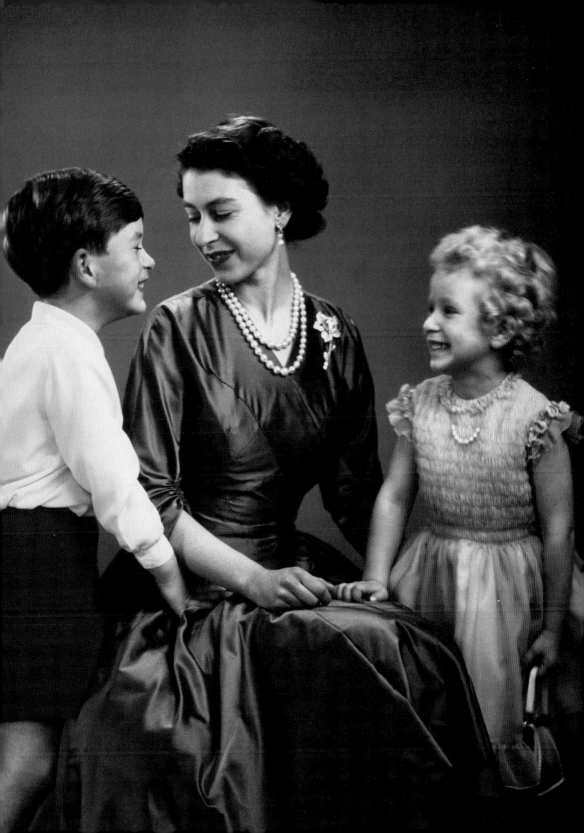

In November 1954, the Queen
accompanied her children to Marcus
Adams's studio for a family sitting.
When speaking of his long association
with the royal family, Adams declared:
'I have had more joy from that family
than from any. They are full of fun.'

[18]
PRINCE CHARLES OF EDINBURGH, QUEEN
ELIZABETH II AND PRINCESS ANNE
THE CHILDREN'S STUDIO, 43 DOVER STREET,
LONDON
MARCUS ADAMS, 6 NOVEMBER 1954

Gelatin silver print, 138 x 100mm
NPG x199859

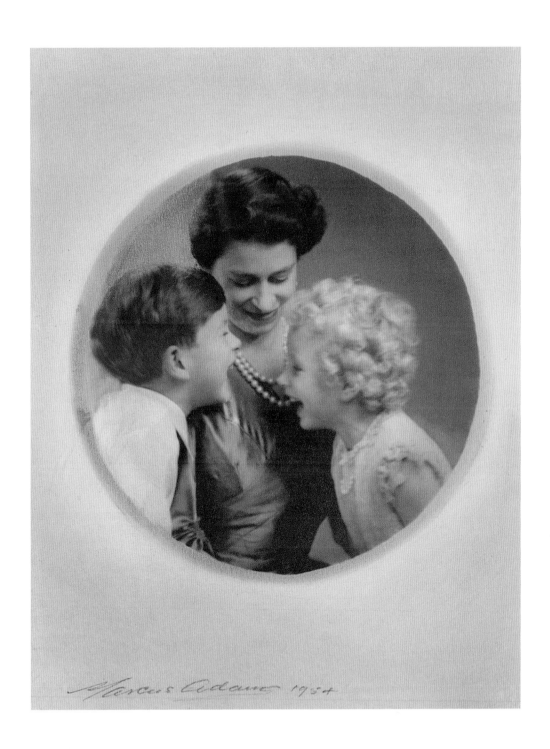

Marcus Adams 1954

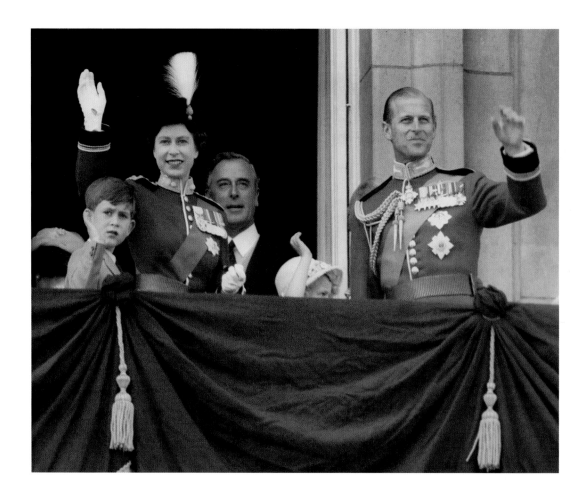

[19]
PRINCE CHARLES OF EDINBURGH, QUEEN
ELIZABETH II, LOUIS MOUNTBATTEN, EARL
MOUNTBATTEN OF BURMA, PRINCESS ANNE
AND PRINCE PHILIP, DUKE OF EDINBURGH
BALCONY OF BUCKINGHAM PALACE, LONDON
STUART HEYDINGER, FOR BIPPA, 31 MAY 1956

Gelatin silver press print, 194 x 239mm
NPG x136397

[20]
PRINCE PHILIP, DUKE OF EDINBURGH,
PRINCESS ANNE, QUEEN ELIZABETH II
AND PRINCE CHARLES OF EDINBURGH
BALMORAL CASTLE, ABERDEENSHIRE
JAMES REID, AUGUST 1955

Gelatin silver print, 497 x 395mm
NPG P1659

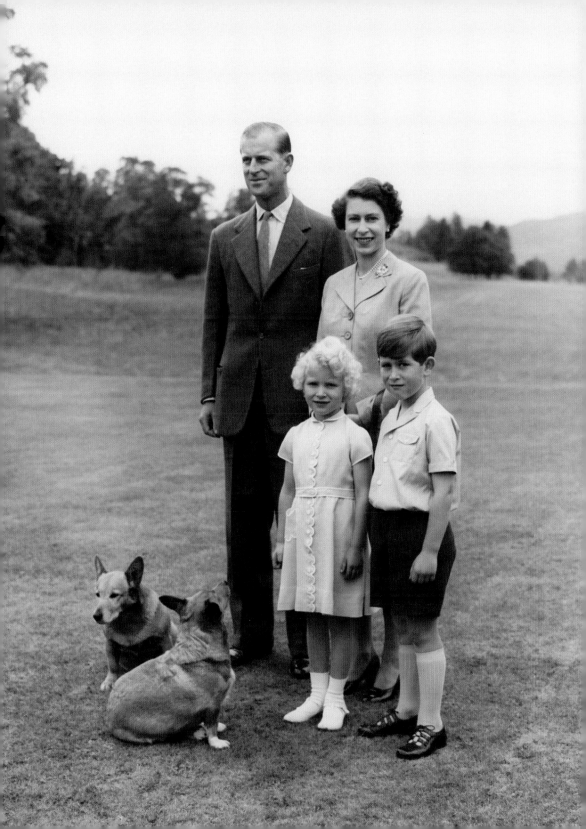

Antony Armstrong Jones was an apprentice to society photographer Baron before opening his first studio on Pimlico Road, London, in 1953. He subsequently became an official royal photographer. This photograph of Princess Anne and Prince Charles represents Snowdon's first royal commission, and was one of 30 photographs taken over two hours, on the occasion of the Prince's eighth birthday.

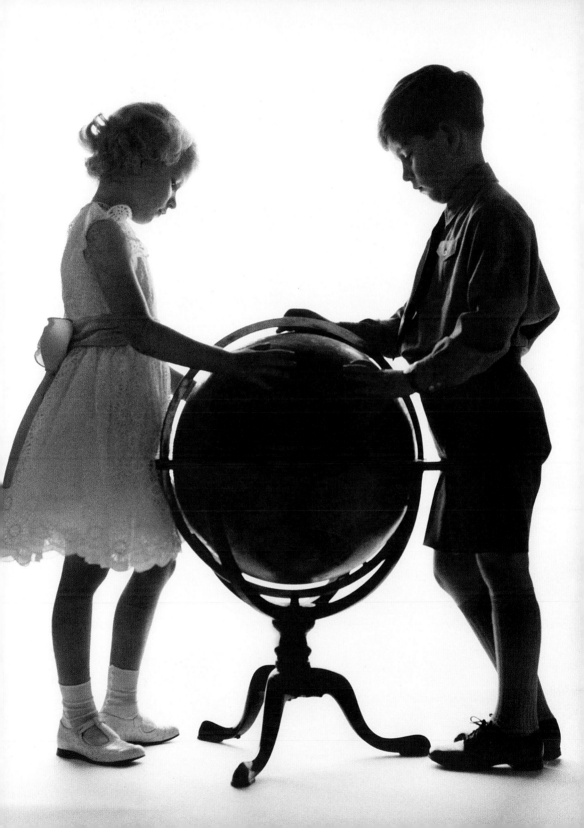

Snowdon photographed the Queen, Prince Philip and their two eldest children in the gardens of Buckingham Palace in 1957. Only 20 minutes were available for the sitting, so he planned it carefully in advance, submitting sketches of compositions for approval. The following year Snowdon met the Queen's sister, Princess Margaret, and the two were married in 1960, after which he was granted the title First Earl of Snowdon.

[22]
PRINCESS ANNE, PRINCE CHARLES OF EDINBURGH, QUEEN ELIZABETH II AND PRINCE PHILIP, DUKE OF EDINBURGH
GARDEN OF BUCKINGHAM PALACE, LONDON
LORD SNOWDON, 10 OCTOBER 1957

Gelatin silver print, 286 x 230mm
NPG x32733

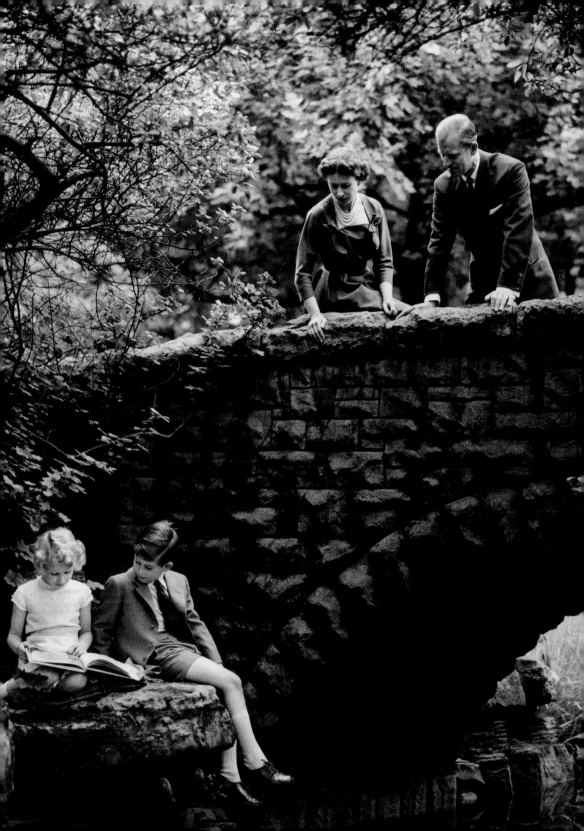

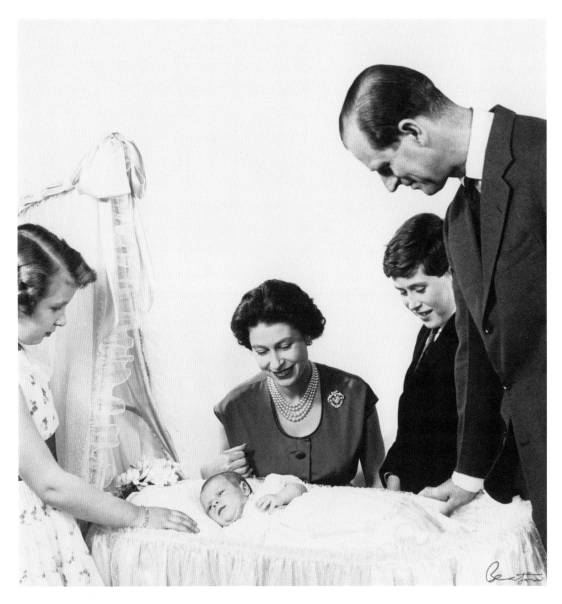

[23]
**PRINCESS ANNE, PRINCE ANDREW, QUEEN
ELIZABETH II, CHARLES, PRINCE OF WALES
AND PRINCE PHILIP, DUKE OF EDINBURGH**
CECIL BEATON, MARCH 1960

Gelatin silver print, 408 x 394mm
NPG P1480

[24]
CHARLES, PRINCE OF WALES
BUCKINGHAM PALACE, LONDON
CECIL BEATON, 1960

Gelatin silver print, 243 x 171mm
NPG x35927

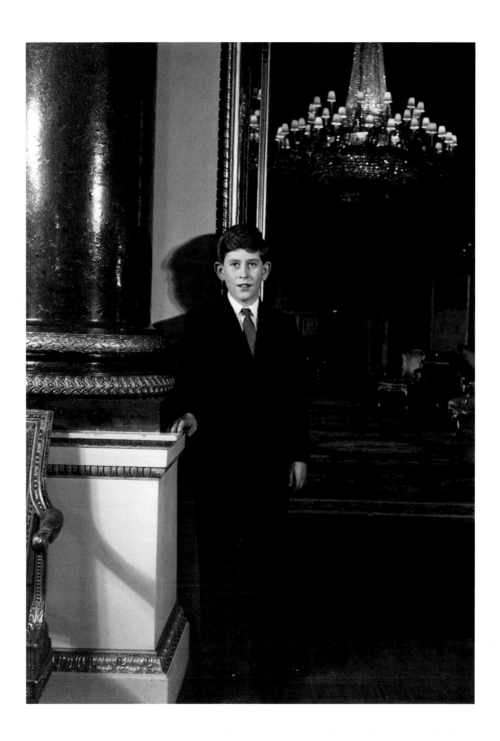

THE
PRINCE
OF
WALES

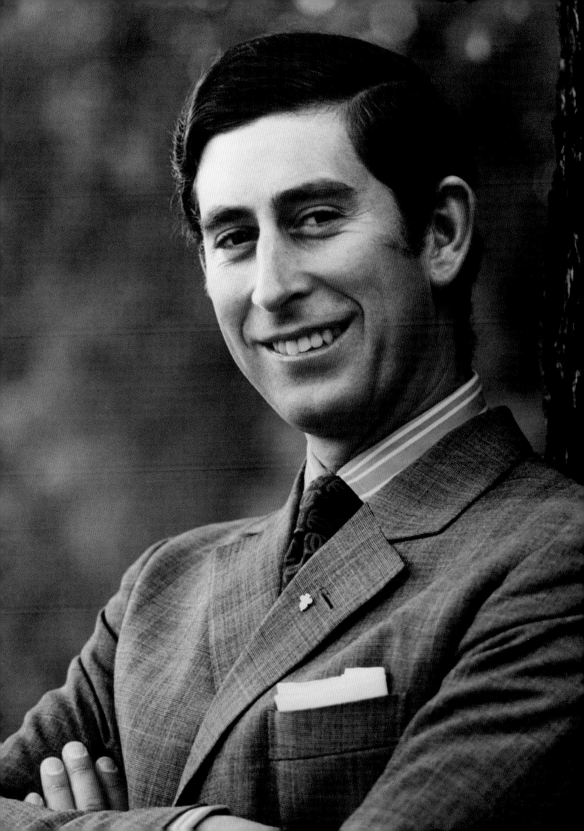

Charles broke royal tradition when he proceeded straight to university after his A-levels, rather than joining the British Armed Forces. In October 1967, he was admitted to Trinity College, Cambridge, where he read history, archaeology and anthropology and on 23 June 1970, Charles became the first British heir apparent to earn a university degree. Charles officially began his investiture as the Prince of Wales on 1 July 1969, when he was crowned by Queen Elizabeth II in a ceremony at Caernarfon Castle, Wales. He took his seat in the House of Lords in 1970, and he made his maiden speech in June 1974, the first royal to speak from the floor since Edward VII in 1884. Charles then served in the Royal Air Force and Royal Navy from 1971 to 1976 before taking on public royal duties, and founding The Prince's Trust in 1976.

[26]
'THE ROYAL FAMILY'
BUCKINGHAM PALACE, LONDON.
PHOTOGRAPHED BEFORE THE STATE
OPENING OF PARLIAMENT
PATRICK LICHFIELD, OCTOBER 1967

Inkjet print, 405 x 304mm
NPG x128494

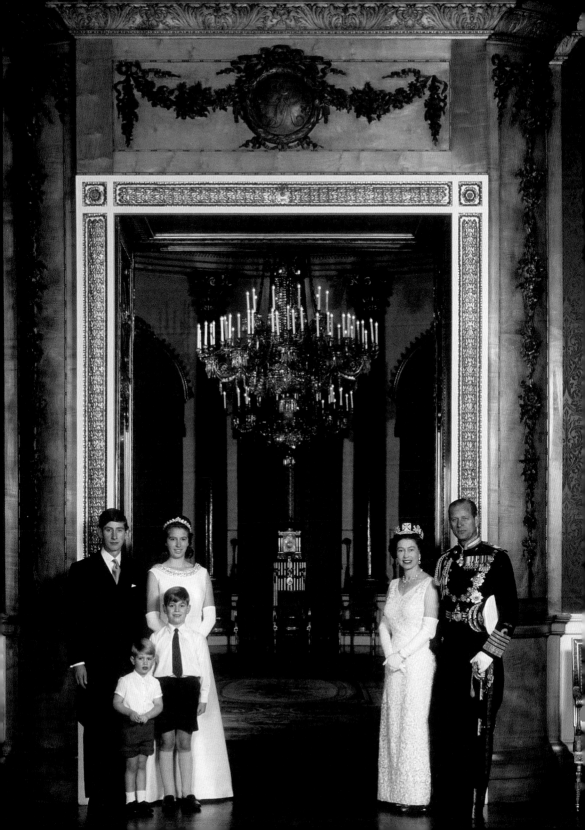

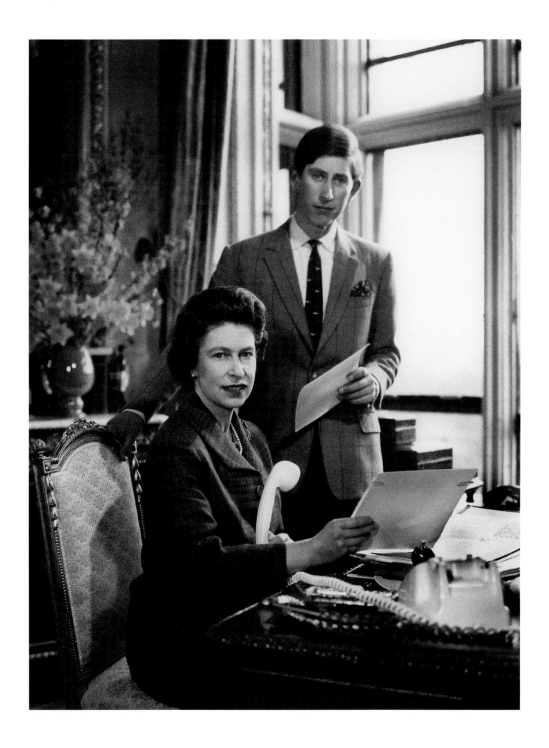

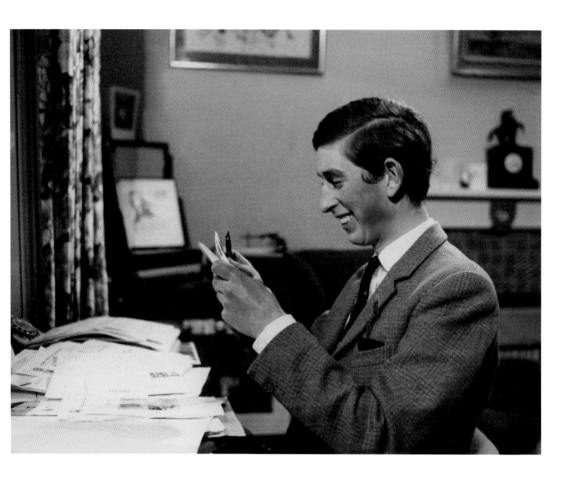

[27]
QUEEN ELIZABETH II AND CHARLES,
PRINCE OF WALES
WINDSOR CASTLE, BERKSHIRE
JOAN WILLIAMS, 1969

Chromogenic print, 199 x 153mm
NPG x200333

[28]
CHARLES, PRINCE OF WALES
TRINITY COLLEGE, CAMBRIDGE UNIVERSITY
JOAN WILLIAMS, 1969

Chromogenic print, 190 x 243mm
NPG x200334

Joan Williams was a distinguished photographer who worked with the BBC covering the royal family for 23 years. In February 1969, President Nixon travelled to Europe on his first foreign trip since taking office. Williams photographed Nixon when he visited Queen Elizabeth II at Buckingham Palace. They are pictured here on a tour of the Marble Hall with Prince Philip and Prince Charles, prior to a luncheon hosted by the Queen in honour of the President, where they were joined by Prime Minister Harold Wilson.

[29]
CHARLES, PRINCE OF WALES, RICHARD NIXON, PRINCE PHILIP, DUKE OF EDINBURGH AND QUEEN ELIZABETH II
BUCKINGHAM PALACE, LONDON
JOAN WILLIAMS, 25 FEBRUARY 1969

Chromogenic print, 240 x 191mm
NPG x200340

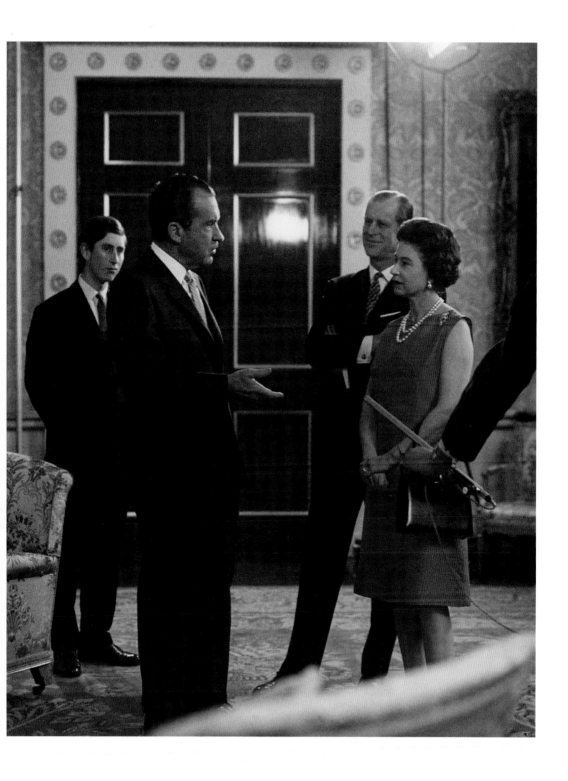

Norman Parkinson was a portrait and fashion photographer whose career spanned seven decades. He became an official royal photographer in 1969 when he photographed Princess Anne's 19th birthday and the investiture portrait of Prince Charles as Prince of Wales. The investiture took place at Caernarfon Castle in Wales on 1 July 1969. Although Prince Charles had been given the title of Prince of Wales and Earl of Chester on 26 July 1958, the investiture was the ceremony that marked the formal presentation of the title. During the ceremony Charles was presented with a golden rod, a mantle, a sword, a girdle, a coronet and a ring by the Welsh secretary of state.

[30]
CHARLES, PRINCE OF WALES
CAERNARFON CASTLE, WALES
NORMAN PARKINSON, 1 JULY 1969

Chromogenic print, 609 x 457mm
NPG x30171

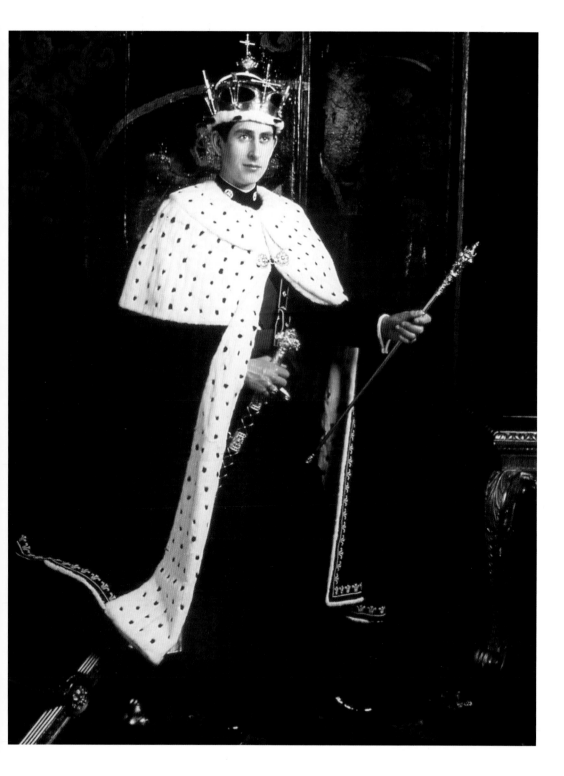

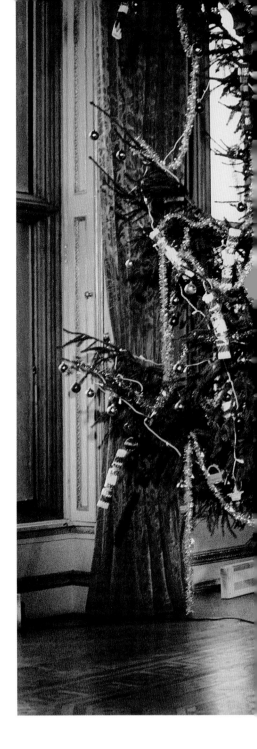

The Royal Family documentary was first aired on BBC One and ITV in 1969, and presented insight into a year in the lives of the Queen and her family, attracting an audience of over 30 million viewers. Joan Williams captured behind-the-scenes images during the making of the documentary for use in the press. Williams continued to document many royal events for the BBC, including state visits and the Queen's Christmas broadcasts.

[31]
'CHRISTMAS AT WINDSOR CASTLE, DECORATING THE TREE'
STATE APARTMENTS AT WINDSOR CASTLE, BERKSHIRE
JOAN WILLIAMS, 1969

Chromogenic print, 195 x 245mm
NPG x199582

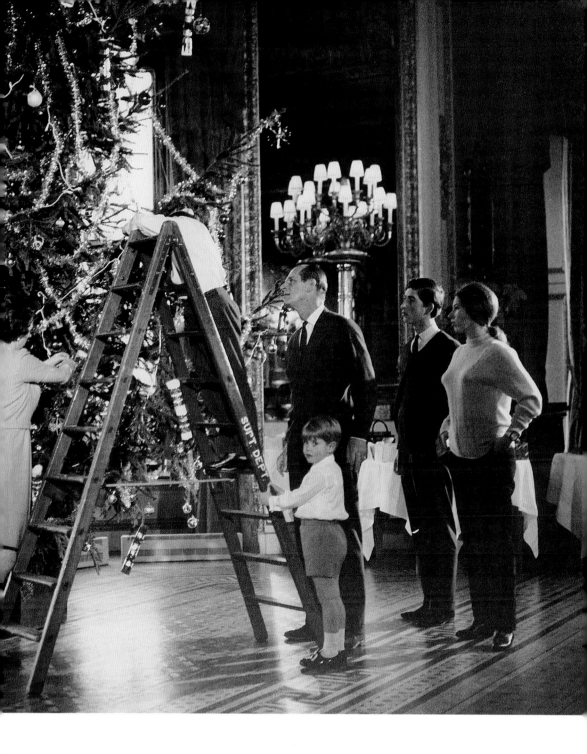

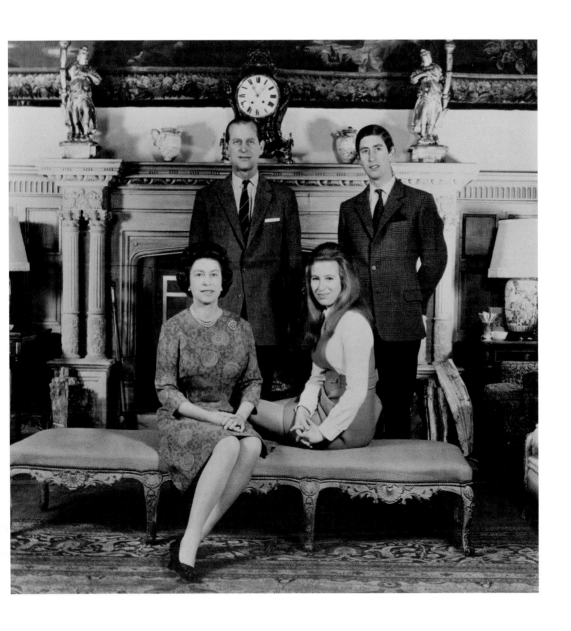

A cousin of the Queen, Patrick Lichfield was an established society and fashion photographer. This group portrait was taken at Windsor Castle to mark the Queen and Prince Philip's silver wedding anniversary. Lichfield's arrangement portrays a family gathering without rigid formality.

[33]
THE OFFICIAL SILVER WEDDING GROUP PHOTOGRAPH OF QUEEN ELIZABETH II AND PRINCE PHILIP, DUKE OF EDINBURGH
WHITE DRAWING ROOM, WINDSOR CASTLE, BERKSHIRE
PATRICK LICHFIELD, 26 DECEMBER 1971

Chromogenic print, 382 x 495mm
NPG x26200

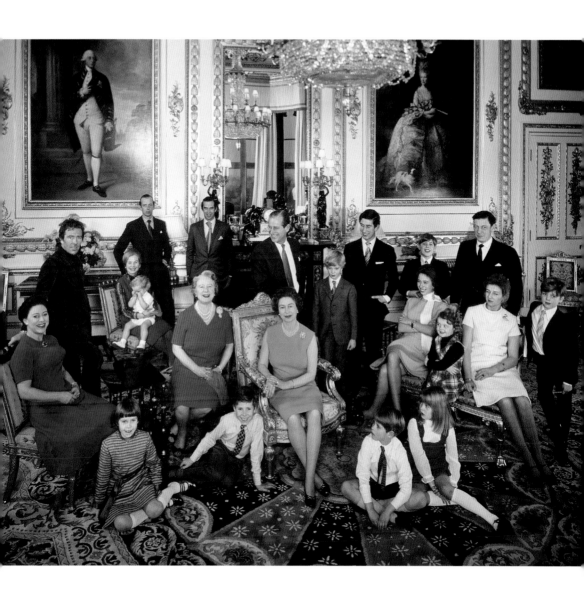

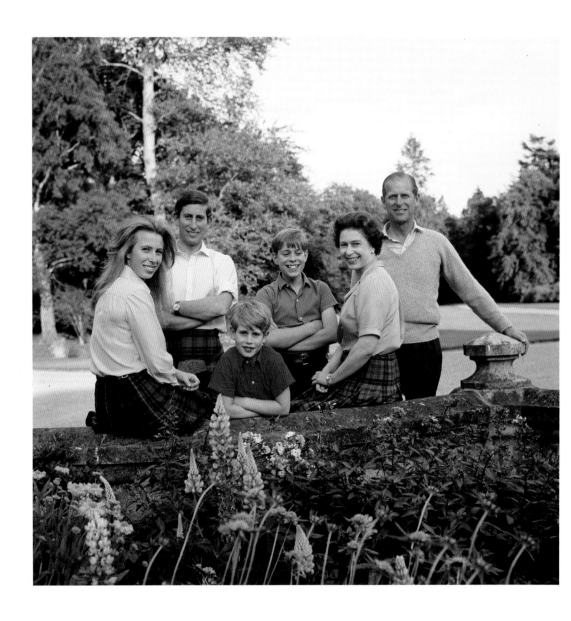

[34]
**QUEEN ELIZABETH II, PRINCE PHILLIP, DUKE OF
EDINBURGH, AND THEIR CHILDREN**
BALMORAL CASTLE, ABERDEENSHIRE
PATRICK LICHFIELD, SUMMER 1972

Chromogenic print, 387 x 490mm
NPG P1578

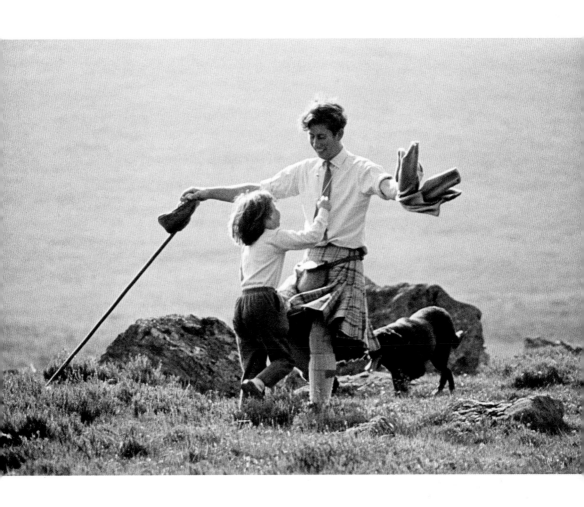

[35]
***LADY SARAH CHATTO AND CHARLES, PRINCE
OF WALES***
BALMORAL CASTLE, ABERDEENSHIRE
PATRICK LICHFIELD, AUGUST 1972

Archival inkjet print, 322 x 482mm
NPG x126907

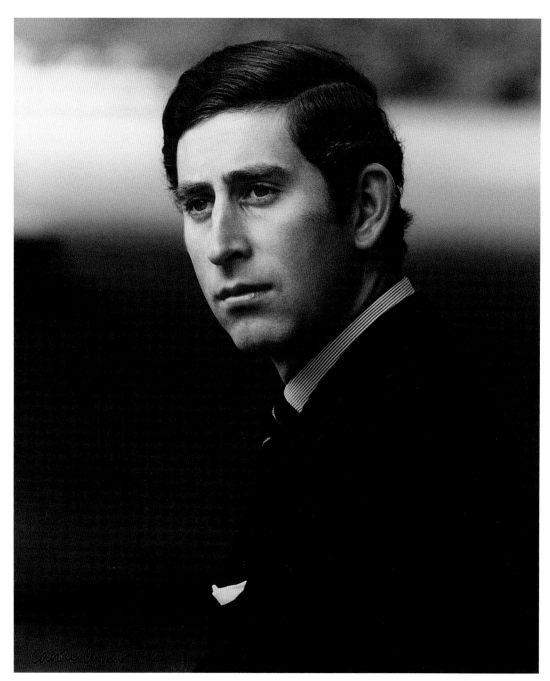

[36]
CHARLES, PRINCE OF WALES
CAROLE CUTNER, 1974

Chromogenic print, 304 x 254mm
NPG x22208

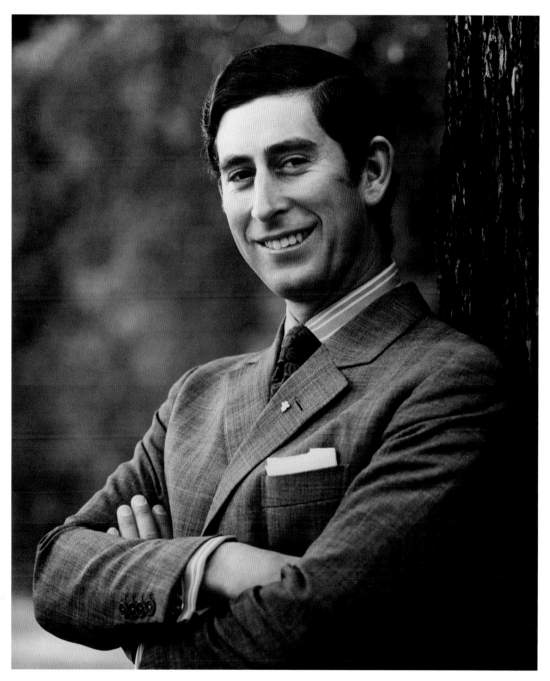

[37]
CHARLES, PRINCE OF WALES
CAROLE CUTNER, NOVEMBER 1974

Chromogenic print, 304 x 254mm
NPG x22209

In September 1971, the year after his investiture as the Prince of Wales, Charles followed in the footsteps of his father, grandfather, and great-grandfathers by starting out on a naval career. Charles began his military service on the guided missile destroyer HMS *Norfolk* in 1971, then went on to serve on two frigates, the HMS *Minerva* from 1972 to 1973, and the HMS *Jupiter* in 1974. Charles is pictured here in his naval uniform during a visit to the Royal Naval College, Greenwich, in 1975 – the same site where Prince Philip had trained and studied in 1948.

[38]
CHARLES, PRINCE OF WALES
ROYAL NAVAL COLLEGE, GREENWICH, LONDON
ERIC GREENHALF, 20 OCTOBER 1975

Gelatin silver print, 392 x 290mm
NPG x12504

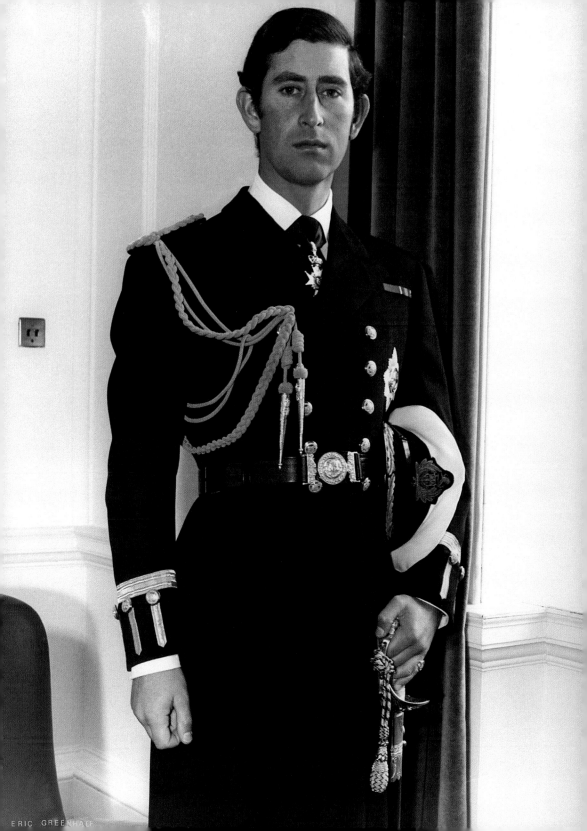

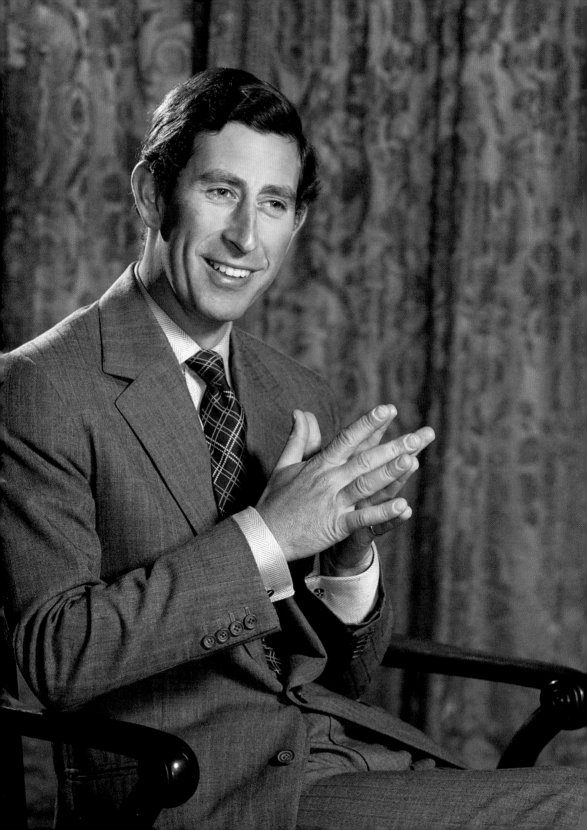

Bern Schwartz was an American businessman who took up photography in the early 1970s as a second career when he was in his sixties. In just a few years, he made memorable portrait studies of many well-known personalities of the time, including artists, politicians and royalty. Schwartz, assisted by his wife, Ronny, often captured his subjects in surroundings reflecting their life, work and personality. After leaving the navy in 1976, Prince Charles founded The Prince's Trust, a charity that supports young people. The following year, Prince Charles, aged 29, sat for this portrait at Buckingham Palace.

[39]
CHARLES, PRINCE OF WALES
BUCKINGHAM PALACE, LONDON
BERN SCHWARTZ, 30 MARCH 1977

Dye transfer print, 280 x 222mm
NPG P1152

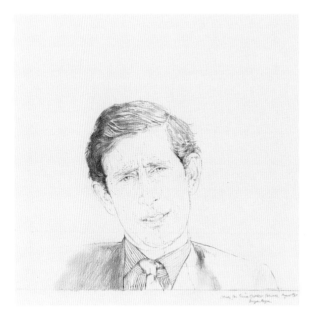

The first painted portrait of Prince Charles to enter the National Portrait Gallery's collection was commissioned by the Gallery's Trustees in 1980. Based on sittings, studies and photographs, this relatively informal portrait shows the Prince in a relaxed position, wearing his polo clothes, a sport he played for 40 years. The following year Bryan Organ was also commissioned to paint the Princess of Wales.

[40]
CHARLES, PRINCE OF WALES
BRYAN ORGAN, 1980

Pencil, 775 x 533mm
NPG 5420

[41]
CHARLES, PRINCE OF WALES
BRYAN ORGAN, 1980

Acrylic on canvas, 1778 x 1782mm
NPG 5365

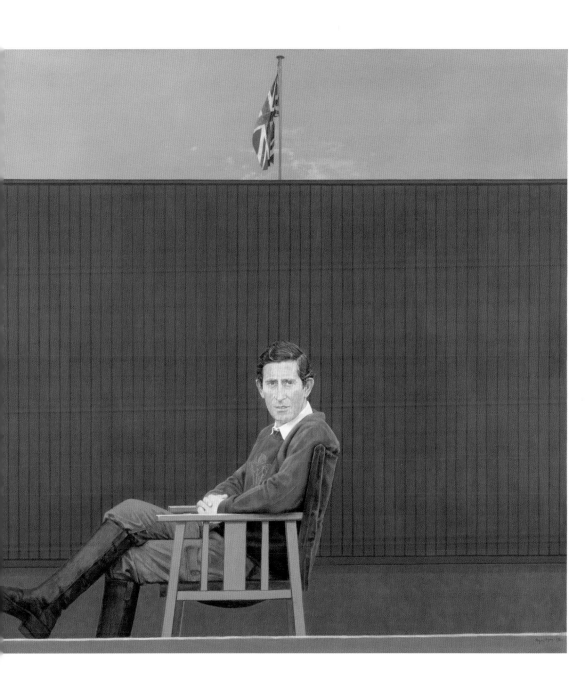

THE
FUTURE
OF THE
MONARCHY

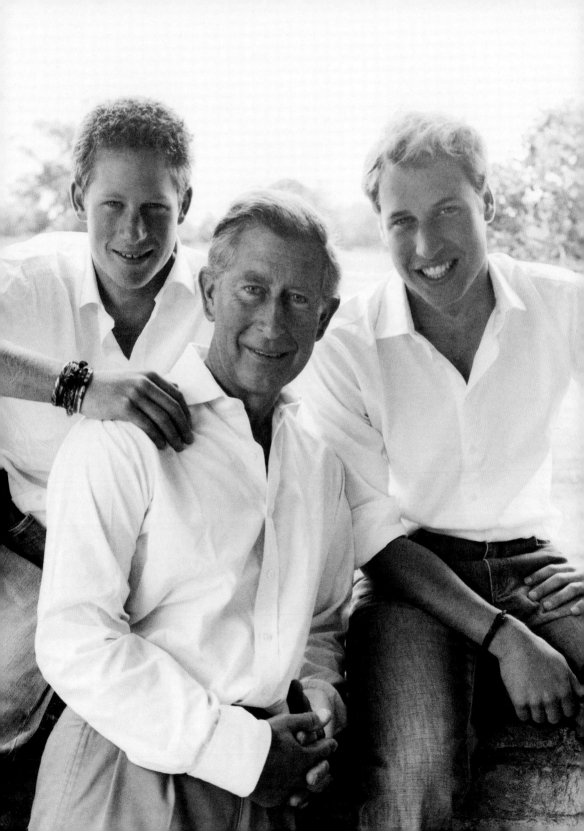

Previous spread (detail)

[42]

**PRINCE HARRY, CHARLES, PRINCE
OF WALES AND PRINCE WILLIAM**
MARIO TESTINO, 2004

Gelatin silver print, 508 x 610mm
NPG P1387

Charles, Prince of Wales, and Diana, Princess of Wales, were married on 29 July 1981. The couple first met in 1977 and went on to have two sons, Prince William in 1982, and Prince Harry in 1984. In August 1996, the 15-year marriage of Charles and Diana ended in divorce. Almost ten years later, on 10 February 2005, Prince Charles and Camilla Parker Bowles announced their engagement, and married later that year on 9 April 2005. Following the death of his mother, Queen Elizabeth II, on 8 September 2022, Charles ascended to the throne to become King Charles III. The following day he paid tribute to the Queen and addressed the nation, stating that: 'I shall endeavour to serve you with loyalty, respect and love, as I have throughout my life.'

In this portrait of the newly married
royal couple, the princess wears an ivory
silk taffeta dress with a 25-foot train
designed by the House of Emanuel. Her
veil was held in place by the Spencer
family diamond tiara. The wedding of the
Prince and Princess of Wales took place
on 29 July 1981 at St Paul's Cathedral.
Patrick Lichfield, a cousin of the Queen,
was the official photographer.

[43]
**CHARLES, PRINCE OF WALES AND DIANA,
PRINCESS OF WALES**
BUCKINGHAM PALACE, LONDON
PATRICK LICHFIELD, JULY 1981

Inkjet print, 304 x 304mm
NPG x128498

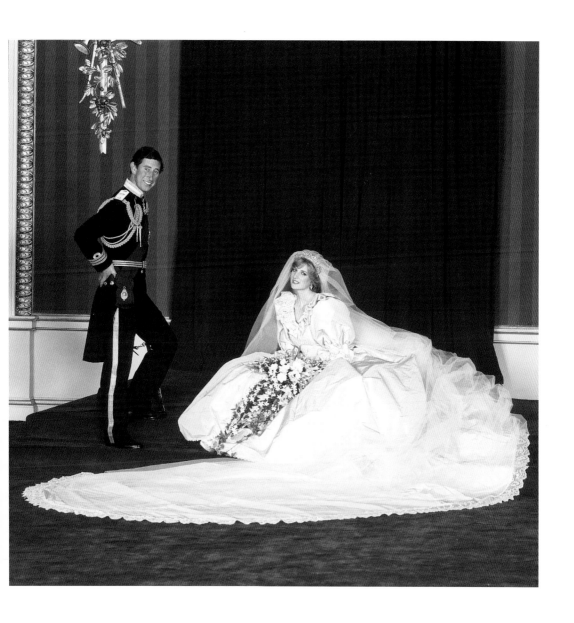

William Arthur Philip Louis is the
eldest son of Charles and Diana and heir
apparent to the throne. He was born
on 12 June 1982 at St Mary's Hospital,
Paddington, and was christened by
Robert Runcie, the Archbishop of
Canterbury, in the Music Room of
Buckingham Palace on 4 August 1982.

[44]
**DIANA, PRINCESS OF WALES AND PRINCE
WILLIAM**
LORD SNOWDON, 1982

Chromogenic print, 266 x 266mm
NPG x29876

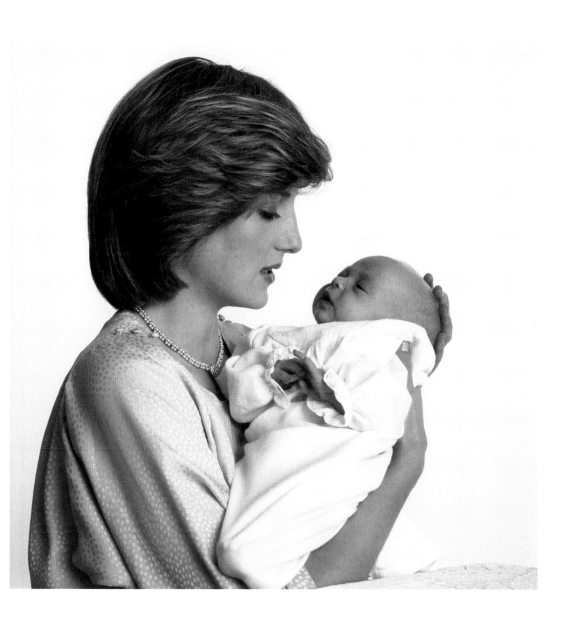

[45]
'QUEEN ELIZABETH II AND PRINCE PHILIP WITH
THEIR GRANDCHILDREN'
BALMORAL CASTLE, ABERDEENSHIRE
YOUSUF KARSH, 1987

Dye transfer print, 972 x 73mm
NPG P543

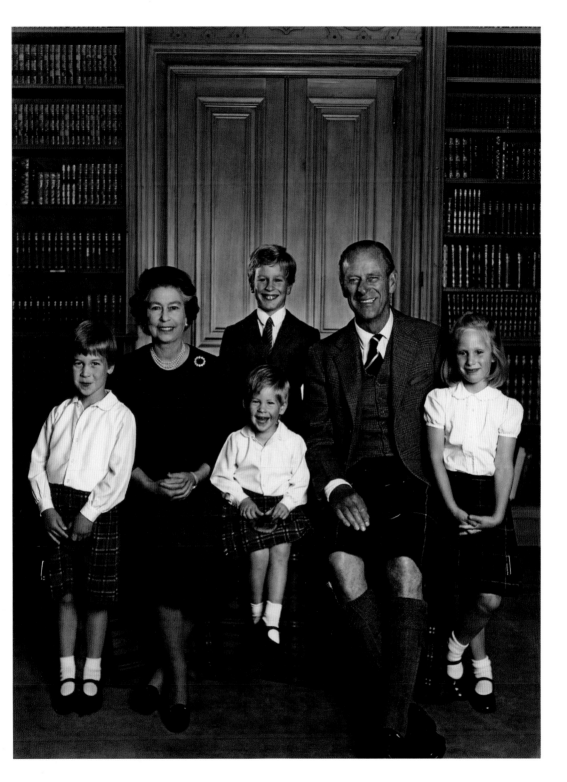

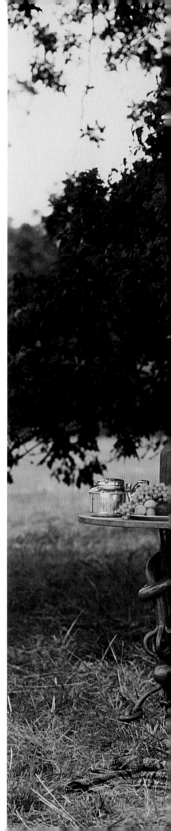

[46]
PRINCE WILLIAM, PRINCE HARRY, CHARLES,
PRINCE OF WALES AND DIANA, PRINCESS
OF WALES
HIGHGROVE, GLOUCESTERSHIRE
LORD SNOWDON, 1991 (PRINTED 2000)

Chromogenic print, 354 x 254mm
NPG x200858

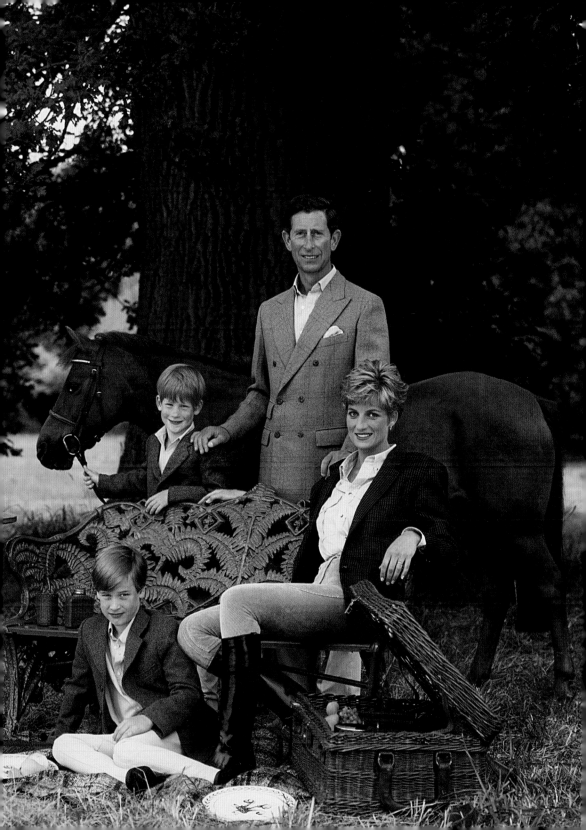

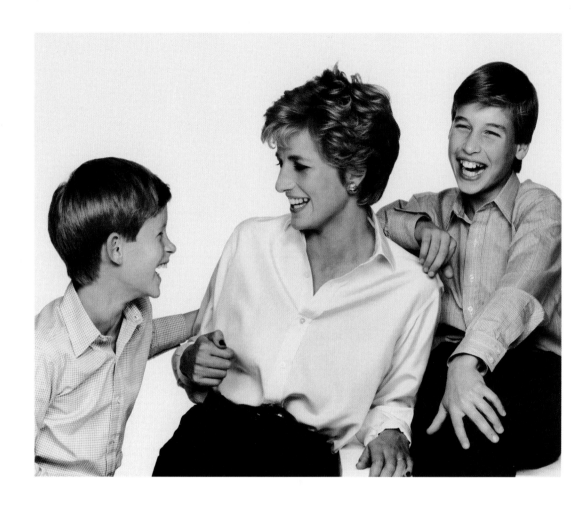

[47]
'DIANA, PRINCESS OF WALES WITH HER SONS'
JOHN SWANNELL, 1994

Inkjet print, 394 x 482mm
NPG P717(16)

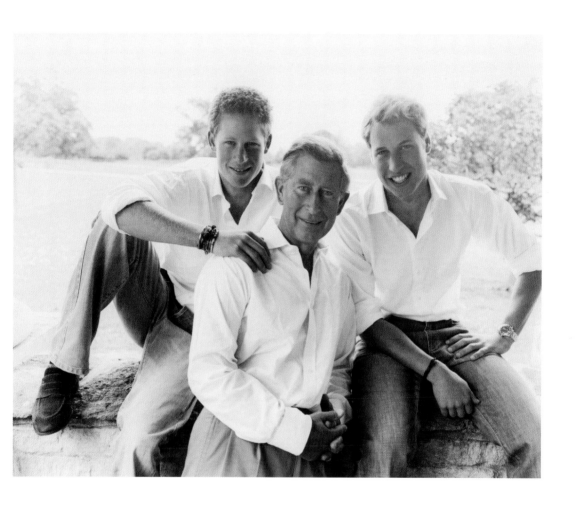

[48]
***PRINCE HARRY, CHARLES, PRINCE
OF WALES AND PRINCE WILLIAM***
MARIO TESTINO, 2004

Gelatin silver print, 508 x 610mm
NPG P1387

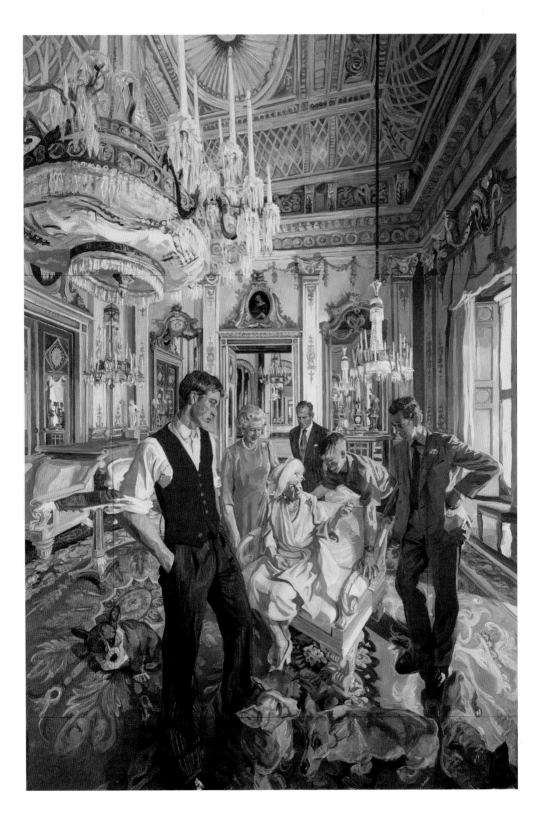

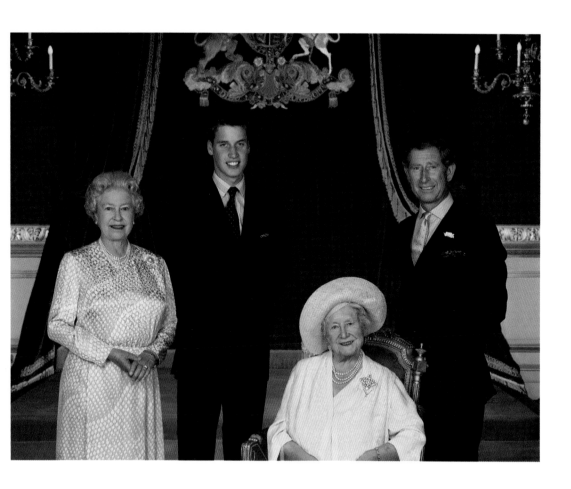

[49]
'THE ROYAL FAMILY: A CENTENARY PORTRAIT'
WHITE DRAWING ROOM, BUCKINGHAM
PALACE, LONDON
JOHN WONNACOTT, 2000

Oil on canvas, 3663 x 2493mm
NPG 6479

[50]
QUEEN ELIZABETH II, PRINCE WILLIAM,
QUEEN ELIZABETH, THE QUEEN MOTHER
AND CHARLES, PRINCE OF WALES
JOHN SWANNELL, 2000

Inkjet print, 298 x 375mm
NPG x88877

Photographed at his home, Highgrove, in Gloucestershire, Prince Charles is shown wearing his favourite coat whilst feeding his rare breed of chickens. The image was published in *Vogue* in February 2002.

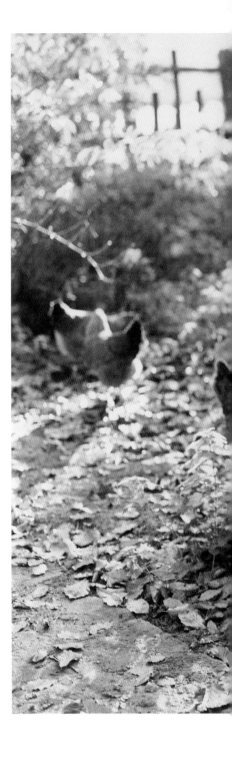

[51]
CHARLES, PRINCE OF WALES
HIGHGROVE, GLOUCESTERSHIRE
MARIO TESTINO, FEBRUARY 2002

Chromogenic print, 405 x 511mm
NPG P1013

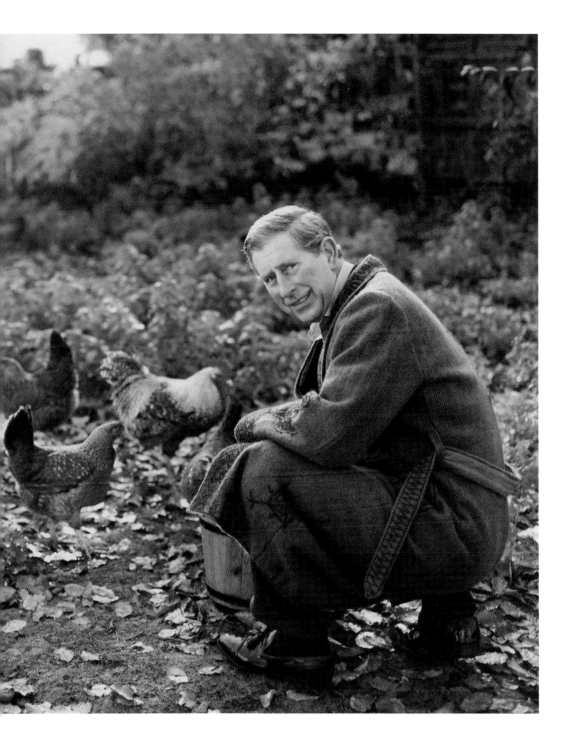

Prince Charles and Camilla, Duchess of Cornwall, are shown here on their first wedding anniversary which they celebrated privately at Birkhall in Scotland. This official photograph, released by Clarence House, and commissioned by *Vogue*, shows Camilla wearing a cornflower blue silk outfit and pearl drop earrings. A cornflower – picked from his gardens at Highgrove, Gloucestershire – can also be seen in Charles's lapel.

[52]
CAMILLA, DUCHESS OF CORNWALL AND CHARLES, PRINCE OF WALES
MARIO TESTINO, 2006

Chromogenic print, 800 x 1050mm
NPG P1987

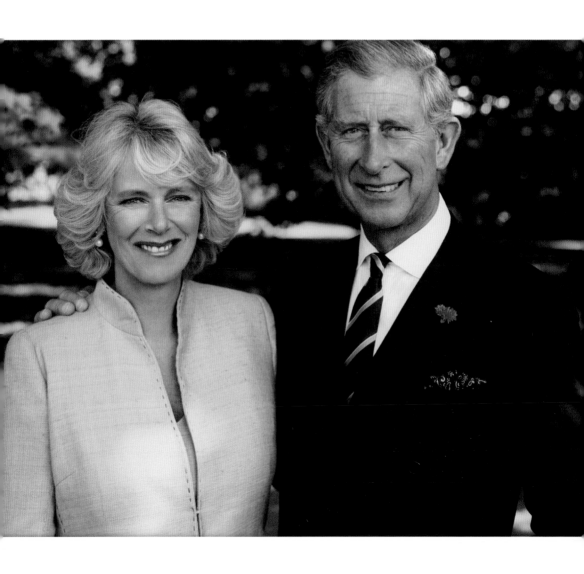

This is the first official oil portrait of
Prince William and Prince Harry. It
represents a unique moment in the lives
of the brothers when they were both
serving officers in the Household Cavalry
(the 'Blues and Royals'). They are shown
wearing regimental dress uniform and
William wears the star and sash of the
Order of the Garter, the highest order of
chivalry in Britain. The painting conveys
what the artist describes as 'an informal
moment within a formal context'.

[53]
PRINCE HARRY AND PRINCE WILLIAM
CLARENCE HOUSE, LONDON
NICKY PHILIPPS, 2009

Oil on canvas, 1374 x 1475mm
NPG 6876

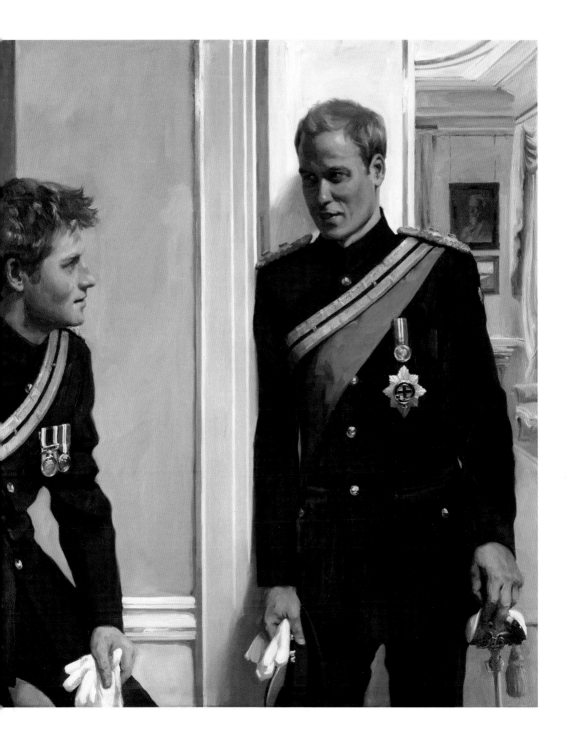

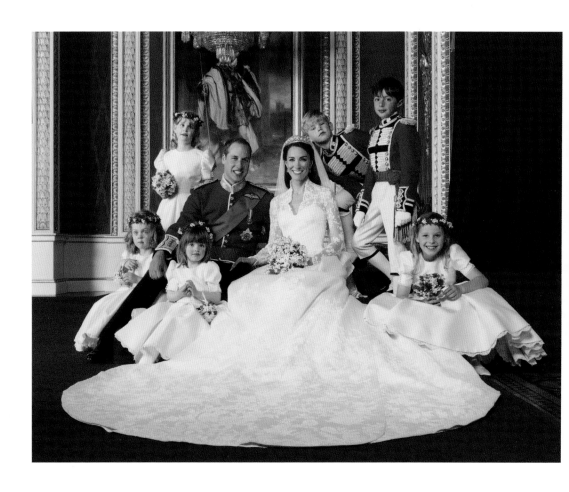

[54]
OFFICIAL WEDDING PHOTOGRAPH OF
PRINCE WILLIAM, DUKE OF CAMBRIDGE
AND CATHERINE, DUCHESS OF CAMBRIDGE
BUCKINGHAM PALACE, LONDON
HUGO BURNAND, 29 APRIL 2011

Inkjet print, 508 x 575mm
NPG x200213

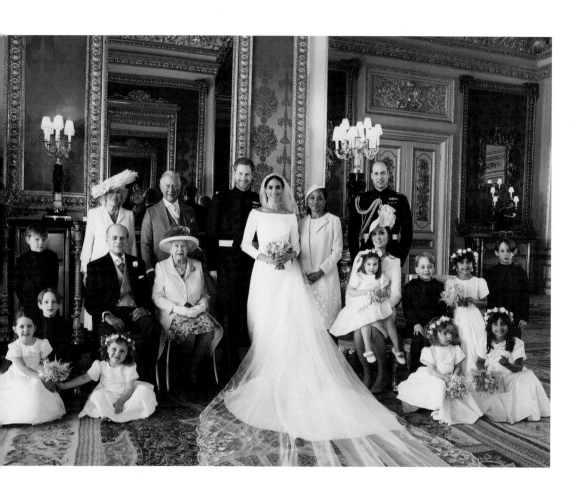

[55]
OFFICIAL WEDDING PHOTOGRAPH OF
PRINCE HARRY, DUKE OF SUSSEX AND
MEGHAN, DUCHESS OF SUSSEX
ALEXI LUBOMIRSKI, 19 MAY 2018

Inkjet print, 420 x 560mm
NPG x200211

George Alexander Louis was born on 22 July 2013 at the Lindo Wing of St Mary's Hospital. As the first child of Prince William and Princess Catherine, Prince George is second in the line of succession to the throne. This photograph depicts four generations of the British monarchy, taken on the day of Prince George's christening which took place at the Chapel Royal at St James's Palace.

[56]
PRINCE GEORGE, PRINCE WILLIAM, QUEEN ELIZABETH II AND CHARLES, PRINCE OF WALES
MORNING ROOM, CLARENCE HOUSE, LONDON
JASON BELL, 23 OCTOBER 2013

Inkjet print, 525 x 405mm
NPG x138989

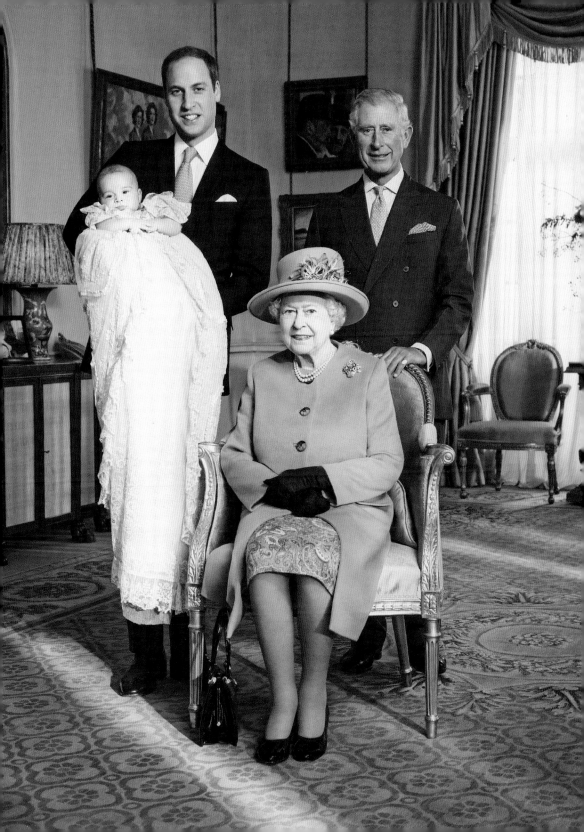

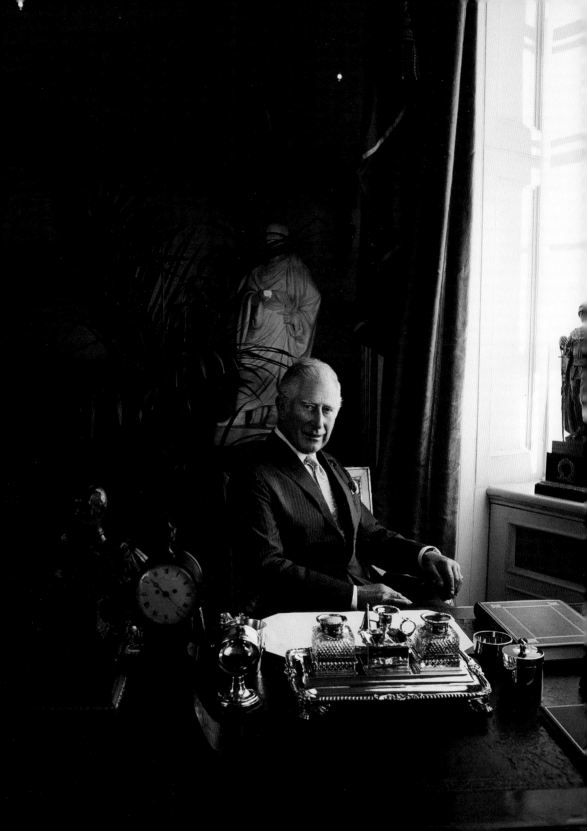

To celebrate the 70th birthday of Prince Charles, fashion photographer Alexi Lubomirski captured a series of photographs of Charles and Camilla to accompany an article for *Vanity Fair*. Here Prince Charles is shown at his desk at Clarence House, his official royal residence in London. Lubomirski also photographed Charles and Camilla in the Garden Room of Clarence House, in front of a French tapestry presented to Queen Victoria by the Emperor Napoleon III.

[57]
CHARLES, PRINCE OF WALES
CLARENCE HOUSE, LONDON
ALEXI LUBOMIRSKI, NOVEMBER 2018

Inkjet print, 697 x 510mm
NPG x201265

[58]
CHARLES, PRINCE OF WALES AND
CAMILLA, DUCHESS OF CORNWALL
GARDEN ROOM, CLARENCE HOUSE,
LONDON
ALEXI LUBOMIRSKI, 2018

Inkjet print, 697 x 510mm
NPG x201266

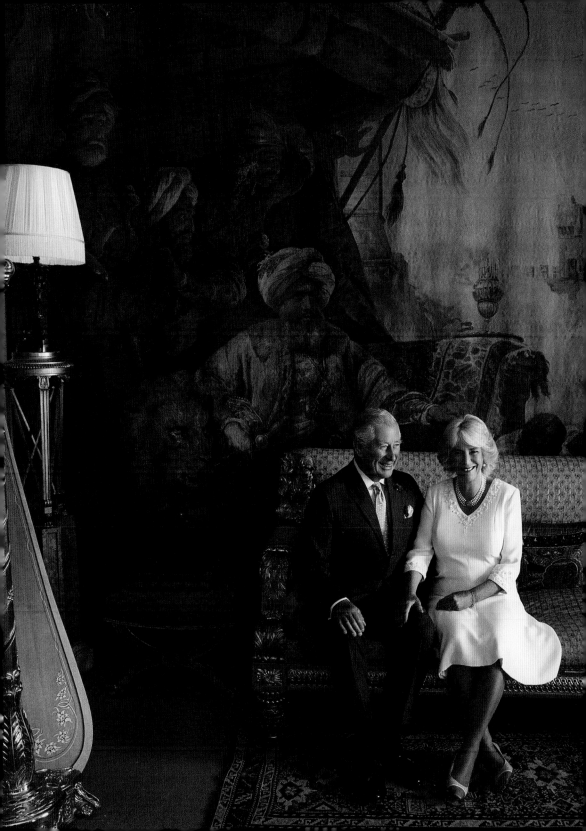

Monumental in scale, closely cropped, and set against a dark background, this charged portrait of Charles suggests an intense expression of both regal composure and human vulnerability. This image was published as the cover of the 4 November 2013 issue of *TIME* magazine, with the title 'The Forgotten Prince'.

[59]
CHARLES, PRINCE OF WALES
BIRKHALL, ABERDEENSHIRE
NADAV KANDER, 20 AUGUST 2013

Chromogenic print, 1565 x 1220mm
NPG P1989

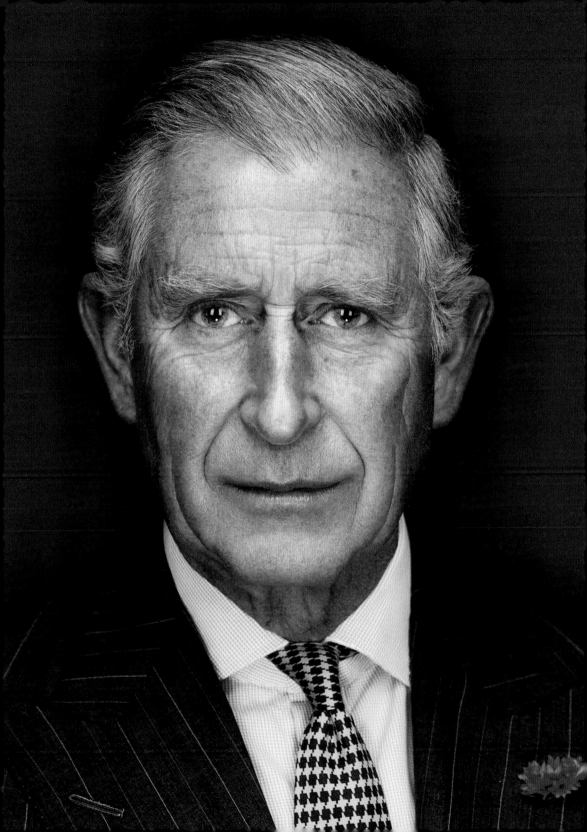

TIMELINE

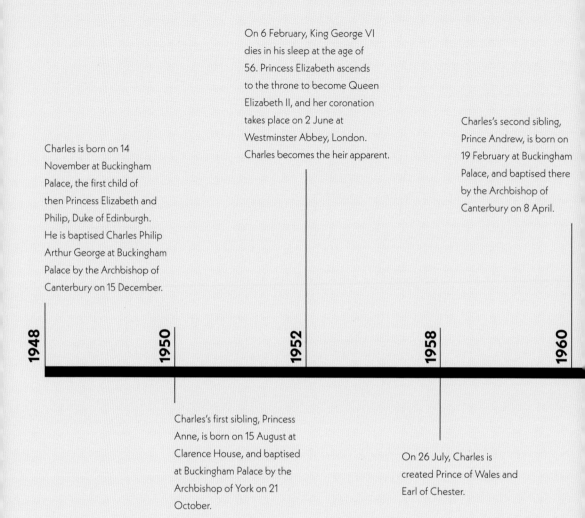

On 6 February, King George VI dies in his sleep at the age of 56. Princess Elizabeth ascends to the throne to become Queen Elizabeth II, and her coronation takes place on 2 June at Westminster Abbey, London. Charles becomes the heir apparent.

Charles's second sibling, Prince Andrew, is born on 19 February at Buckingham Palace, and baptised there by the Archbishop of Canterbury on 8 April.

Charles is born on 14 November at Buckingham Palace, the first child of then Princess Elizabeth and Philip, Duke of Edinburgh. He is baptised Charles Philip Arthur George at Buckingham Palace by the Archbishop of Canterbury on 15 December.

1948

1950

1952

1958

1960

Charles's first sibling, Princess Anne, is born on 15 August at Clarence House, and baptised at Buckingham Palace by the Archbishop of York on 21 October.

On 26 July, Charles is created Prince of Wales and Earl of Chester.

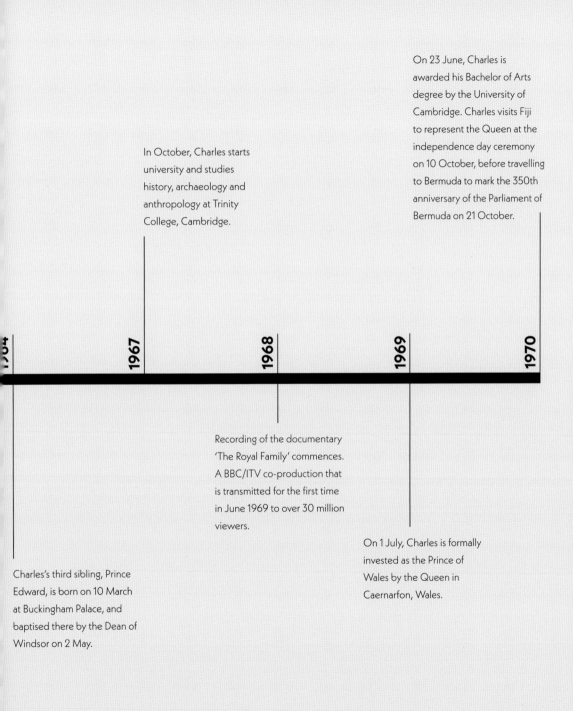

In October, Charles starts
university and studies
history, archaeology and
anthropology at Trinity
College, Cambridge.

On 23 June, Charles is
awarded his Bachelor of Arts
degree by the University of
Cambridge. Charles visits Fiji
to represent the Queen at the
independence day ceremony
on 10 October, before travelling
to Bermuda to mark the 350th
anniversary of the Parliament of
Bermuda on 21 October.

1967

1968

1969

1970

Recording of the documentary
'The Royal Family' commences.
A BBC/ITV co-production that
is transmitted for the first time
in June 1969 to over 30 million
viewers.

On 1 July, Charles is formally
invested as the Prince of
Wales by the Queen in
Caernarfon, Wales.

Charles's third sibling, Prince
Edward, is born on 10 March
at Buckingham Palace, and
baptised there by the Dean of
Windsor on 2 May.

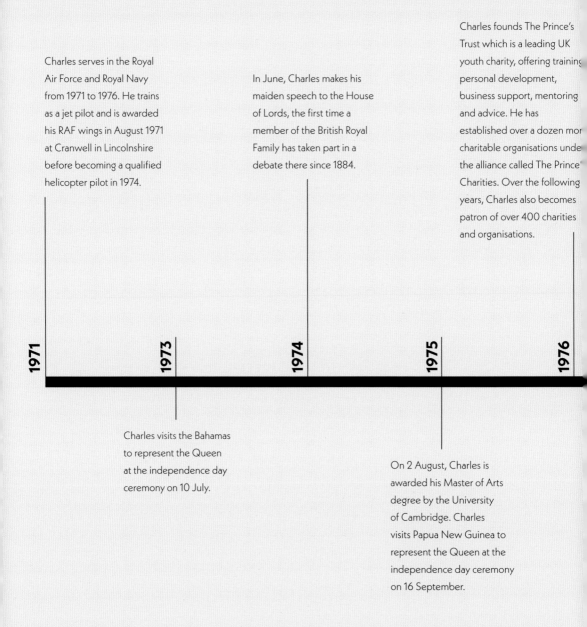

Charles serves in the Royal Air Force and Royal Navy from 1971 to 1976. He trains as a jet pilot and is awarded his RAF wings in August 1971 at Cranwell in Lincolnshire before becoming a qualified helicopter pilot in 1974.

In June, Charles makes his maiden speech to the House of Lords, the first time a member of the British Royal Family has taken part in a debate there since 1884.

Charles founds The Prince's Trust which is a leading UK youth charity, offering training, personal development, business support, mentoring and advice. He has established over a dozen more charitable organisations under the alliance called The Prince' Charities. Over the following years, Charles also becomes patron of over 400 charities and organisations.

1971

1973

1974

1975

1976

Charles visits the Bahamas to represent the Queen at the independence day ceremony on 10 July.

On 2 August, Charles is awarded his Master of Arts degree by the University of Cambridge. Charles visits Papua New Guinea to represent the Queen at the independence day ceremony on 16 September.

On 24 February, Buckingham Palace announces the engagement of Prince Charles and Diana Spencer. On 29 July, an international audience of three-quarters of a billion watches the televised royal wedding, which takes place at St Paul's Cathedral. Diana is given the title Princess of Wales.

Charles visits Brunei to represent the Queen at the independence day ceremony on 24 February. On 15 September, Charles and Diana welcome their second son, Prince Harry, who is also born at St Mary's Hospital, London. He is baptised Henry Charles Albert David at Windsor Castle on 21 December.

1981

1982

1983

1984

Charles visits Zimbabwe to represent the Queen at the independence day ceremony on 18 April. Charles publishes a children's book 'The Old Man of Lochnagar'.

On 21 June Charles and Diana welcome their first son, Prince William, who is born at the Lindo Wing of St Mary's Hospital, London. He is baptised William Arthur Philip Louis at Buckingham Palace on 4 August.

In March and April, Charles, Diana and William visit Australia and New Zealand on their first royal tour as a family.

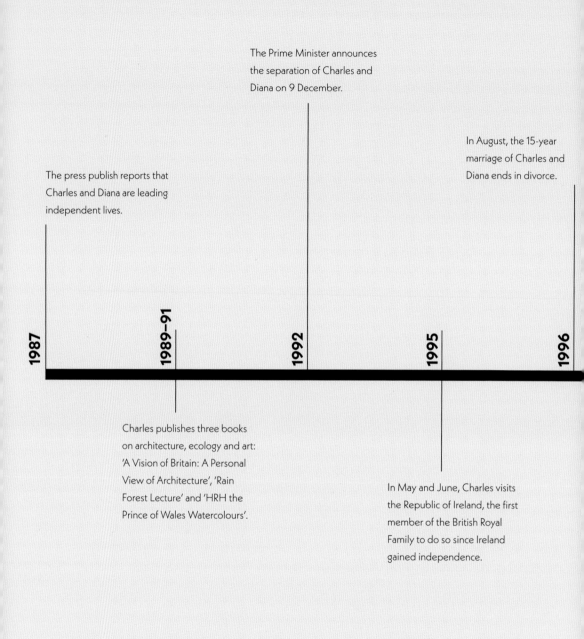

The Prime Minister announces the separation of Charles and Diana on 9 December.

In August, the 15-year marriage of Charles and Diana ends in divorce.

The press publish reports that Charles and Diana are leading independent lives.

1987

1989–91

1992

1995

1996

Charles publishes three books on architecture, ecology and art: 'A Vision of Britain: A Personal View of Architecture', 'Rain Forest Lecture' and 'HRH the Prince of Wales Watercolours'.

In May and June, Charles visits the Republic of Ireland, the first member of the British Royal Family to do so since Ireland gained independence.

On 10 February, Prince Charles announces his engagement to Camilla Parker Bowles. On 9 April Prince Charles marries Camilla in a civil ceremony at Windsor Guildhall. Camilla is given the title Duchess of Cornwall.

To celebrate the Queen's Diamond Jubilee, Charles and Camilla visit Australia, Canada, New Zealand and Papua New Guinea.

2005

2010

2011

2012

Charles represents the Queen at the opening ceremony of the 2010 Commonwealth Games in Delhi on 3 October. Charles publishes 'Harmony: A New Way of Looking at Our World' which articulates the principles and underlying philosophies of his charities.

Charles represents the Queen at the Hong Kong handover ceremony on 1 July. On 31 August, the death of Diana, Princess of Wales, in a car accident in Paris, provokes widespread grief and tributes.

On 29 April, Charles's first son, Prince William, marries Kate Middleton at Westminster Abbey, London. Catherine is given the title Duchess of Cambridge.

Charles becomes a grandfather
for the first time when William
and Catherine welcome their
first child, Prince George, on
22 July. Charles represents
the Queen for the first time
at the Commonwealth Heads
of Government meeting in
Colombo on 15 November.

William and Catherine welcome
their third child, Prince Louis, on
23 April. On 19 May, Charles's
second son, Prince Harry, marries
Meghan Markle at St George's
Chapel at Windsor Castle.
Meghan is given the title Duchess
of Sussex, and in the absence of
her father, is escorted down the
aisle by Charles. Leaders of the
Commonwealth vote that Charles
will succeed the Queen as Head
of the Commonwealth; he takes
up the role on 8 September 2022.

Charles remotely opens the
Nightingale Hospital, London,
which was built to deal with
the Covid-19 emergency.

2013

2015

2018

2019

2020

William and Catherine welcome
their second child, Princess
Charlotte, on 2 May. Charles
and Camilla visit the Republic of
Ireland later that month.

On 7 March, the Queen hosts
an event at Buckingham Palace
to mark the 50th anniversary
of Charles's investiture as the
Prince of Wales. Later that month
Charles and Camilla visit Cuba,
making them the first members
of the British Royal Family in
history to visit the country. Harry
and Meghan welcome their
first child, Archie Mountbatten-
Windsor on 6 May.

Charles stands in for the Queen for the first time during the state opening of Parliament on 10 May to deliver the Queen's Speech. The delegation of the role, one of the Queen's most important duties, was seen by many as a sign that a transition of the monarchy was underway.

This book is published to mark the coronation on 6 May of King Charles III.

2021

MAY **2022**

SEPTEMBER **2022**

2023

On 9 April Charles's father, Prince Philip, dies at the age of 99. He was the longest serving royal consort in British history and was married to Queen Elizabeth II for 75 years. Harry and Meghan welcome their second child, Lilibet Mountbatten-Windsor on 4 June. Charles visits Barbados to represent the Queen at celebrations to mark their transition into a parliamentary republic on 29 November.

On 8 September Charles's mother, Queen Elizabeth II, dies peacefully with her family by her bedside at the age of 96. She was the longest reigning monarch in British history. That same day Prince Charles ascends to the throne to become King Charles III and Camilla is given the title Queen Consort. Prince William and Catherine, Duchess of Cambridge, are given the titles the Prince and Princess of Wales. On 9 September, Charles addresses the nation, and pays tribute to his mother.

BIBLIOGRAPHY

The captions accompanying the images draw on material from a range of National Portrait Gallery publications and online resources, with further research contributed by curators Clare Freestone and Georgia Atienza.

National Portrait Gallery: A Portrait of Britain (2014)

Cannadine, Sir David, *Tudors to Windsors: British Royal Portraits* (2018)

Moorhouse, Paul, *The Queen: Art and Image* (2011)

Muir, Robin, *VOGUE 100: A Century of Style* (2016)

Saywell, David, *Complete Illustrated Catalogue* (2004)

Shulman, Alexandra, *Elizabeth II: Princess, Queen, Icon* (2022)

Williamson, David, *Kings and Queens* (2010)

npg.org.uk

PICTURE CREDITS

pp. 2, 83 © National Portrait Gallery, London. Commissioned, 1980

pp. 8, 76 © Carole J Cutner. Purchased, 1983

p. 12 © National Portrait Gallery, London. Purchased 2011

pp. 13, 115 © Nadav Kander. Purchased, 2015

pp. 15, 27 © Cecil Beaton / Camera Press. Given by Eileen Hose, 1986

p. 17 © Cecil Beaton / Camera Press. Acquired from Cecil Beaton, 1977

p. 20 © Cecil Beaton / Camera Press. Purchased 1977

p. 21 © Baron / Camera Press. Purchased 1977

p. 22 © Baron / Camera Press. Acquired as part of Elizabeth II exhibition, 1986

p. 23 © Baron / Camera Press. Purchased 1977

p. 25 © Estate of Marcus Adams / Camera Press. Transferred from Hulton Picture Library, 1986

p. 29 © Estate of Marcus Adams / Camera Press. Purchased 1977

pp. 30–31 © Karsh. Given by the photographer, Yousuf Karsh, 1987

p. 33 © Estate of Marcus Adams / Camera Press. Given by Terence Pepper, 2014

p. 34 © reserved; collection National Portrait Gallery, London. Purchased, 1990

p. 35 © National Portrait Gallery, London. Purchased 1977

p. 37 © Studio Lisa / Hulton Archive / Getty Images. Given by Mr Ford Hill and the American Friends of the National Portrait Gallery Foundation, Inc., 2015

p. 41 © Studio Lisa / Hulton Archive / Getty Images. Given by Mr Ford Hill and the American Friends of the National Portrait Gallery Foundation, Inc., 2015

Published in Great Britain by
National Portrait Gallery Publications
National Portrait Gallery
St Martin's Place
London WC2H 0HE

Every purchase supports the National
Portrait Gallery, London
www.npg.org/publications

Text pp.9–14 by Alison Smith, Chief Curator,
National Portrait Gallery, London.

Front cover: *Charles, Prince of Wales* by Nadav
Kander, 20 August 2013

Back cover: *Charles, Prince of Wales and
Camilla, Duchess of Cambridge* by Alexi
Lubomirski, 2018

ISBN 978-1-85514-577-1

A catalogue record for this book is available
from the British Library.

10 9 8 7 6 5 4 3 2 1

Director of Commercial: Anna Starling
Publishing Manager: Kara Green
Production Controller: Priti Kothary
Proofreader: Sara Harrison
Design: Daniela Rocha
Printed in Italy by Printer Trento
Origination by DL Imaging

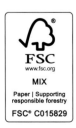

FSC
www.fsc.org
MIX
Paper | Supporting
responsible forestry
FSC® C015829